Praise from Global Business Leaders

"This very helpful book ... who
you are and what you ... to
focus and concentrate ... atter
most in moving you qui ... ladder."

Brian Tracy
Success Expert
World Best-Selling Author

"The Career Acceleration Process that the authors present is a clear, practical, thorough guide to personal and career development covering all the essential factors in an easy-to-remember, seven-step approach."

Harvey Schachter
Globe and Mail
Management Columnist

"An easy read...and very insightful. This book captures the best leadership ideas in an engaging, informative style. A must read for people at any stage of their careers."

Susan Stern
National Executive Director
Weizmann Canada

"7 Steps to Supercharge Your Career is a great read! This book uses everyday language, simple stages and steps, and a checklist to help operationalize learning, with a summary at the end of every chapter. The examples were real and pragmatic. Congratulations!"

Jennifer Sondergaard
Executive Advisor
International Banking Operations

"7 Steps to Supercharge Your Career is enthusiasm-invoking, thought-provoking, and action-inducing all at once. This book is chock full of guidance that will help anyone identify and achieve his or her goals. The authors have tackled the entire process needed to get to the top and laid each piece bare for us to consider. I was truly blown away by the scope of what they tackled and spelled out for us."

Nancy McKinley
International HR Consultant

"7 Steps to Supercharge your Career is full of practical, real world suggestions that anyone can follow. Applying the career acceleration process will provide the reader with all the tools needed to fulfill their career goals. This is a book that I personally recommend that every business should provide for their staff, the results I am sure will be very positive."

Greg Boyle
Managing Partner [Ottawa]
Stonewood Group
Executive Search and Recruitment

"This book is a great read for anyone who is looking to fulfill their career potential while adding material value to their organization. The Career Acceleration Process is a simple, powerful and practical system to empower you to achieve!"

David Reiling
CEO
Sunrise Banks USA

"7 Steps to Supercharge Your Career" is an interesting read that provides a very real and pragmatic approach for achieving career success. A great book regardless of where you are in your career journey!"

Mark Lambert
Managing Director
Global Consulting Company

7 STEPS TO SUPERCHARGE YOUR CAREER

Executive Insights to Move Up Fast

David Booker
and
Sharon Letovsky, PhD

CCI Publications
Ottawa, Canada

CCI Publications

Ottawa, Ontario

Canada

Cover by Chris Jones

Layout by Jesse Caldwell

Edited by Anita Flegg, The Sharp Quill Ltd.

Career Assessment by Steve Letovsky, LBC Consulting

Index by Clive Pyne, Clive Pyne Book Indexing services

Library and Archives Canada Cataloguing in Publication

Booker, David, 1962-, author
    7 steps to supercharge your career : executive insights
to move up fast / David Booker, Sharon Letovsky, PhD.

Includes index.

Previously published under title: 7 steps to the boardroom.

Issued in print and electronic formats.

ISBN 978-0-9868038-4-0 (pbk.).--ISBN 978-0-9868038-2-6 (ebook)

    1. Career development. 2. Performance. I. Letovsky, Sharon, author

II. Booker, David, 1962- 7 steps to the boardroom. III. Title. IV. Title: Seven

steps to supercharge your career.

HF5386.B65 2014   650.14   C2014-901040-0

                                                 C2014-901041-9

Dedications

From David

To my mum and dad, Janet and Michael, and to my sister Kim, for giving me the foundation from which to develop my potential. Good job.

From Sharon

To my parents, Rose and Julius Letovsky, who have encouraged, supported, and loved me through all my wonderful and creative adventures. I love you and thank you from the bottom of my heart.

Acknowledgements

From David

I wish to thank Julie, my life partner, who is my inspiration and without whom I would never have fulfilled any of my goals. I wish to thank our children Luke, Amy, Hayley, and Sam, for providing infinite love in my life and for spending all my money. I wish to thank everyone who has contributed to my experiences; a piece of each of you is in this book.

From Sharon

I wish to thank the clients, colleagues, teachers, and mentors who have inspired and guided me over the years. I particularly want to thank my three daughters, Cynthia, Stefanie, and Alison. As you grew, you helped me to learn more about management and leadership than I could ever learn in school. I am so proud of the fine adults you have become.

Contents

The Career Acceleration Process   **1**

Ground Zero   **11**

Stage One: Discovery   **19**

Step 1: Functional   **21**

My Attributes   **22**

Powering Up   **37**

Step 2: Collaborative   **51**

Influencing How Others See You   **51**

How To Work With Others   **64**

Stage Two: Development   **75**

Step 3: Progressive   **77**

Step 4: Constructive   **97**

Stage Three: Delivery   **119**

Step 5: Leadership   **121**

Leading People   **122**

Leading Business   **148**

Step 6: Executive   **175**

Stage Four: Design   **195**

Step 7: Visionary   **197**

Conclusion   **213**

Origins of the 7 Steps   **215**

Appendices   **223**

-A- CAP Assessment   **225**

-B- How to Interpret Your Scores   **229**

Index   **237**

THE CAREER ACCELERATION PROCESS

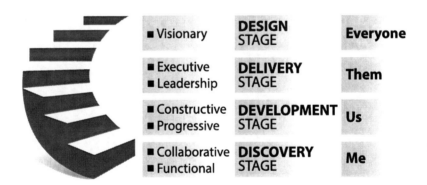

■ Visionary	**DESIGN** STAGE	**Everyone**
■ Executive ■ Leadership	**DELIVERY** STAGE	**Them**
■ Constructive ■ Progressive	**DEVELOPMENT** STAGE	**Us**
■ Collaborative ■ Functional	**DISCOVERY** STAGE	**Me**

THE CAREER ACCELERATION PROCESS

IF YOU ARE INTERESTED in being more satisfied in your job, happier in your home life, more productive, and rising to the level of responsibility that matches your potential, read on.

In our many years of working with people at all levels around the world, we have met many who are happy and satisfied. We have also discovered that far too many people are struggling in their careers and not realizing their potential. For some, their job has lost its shine or its purpose. For others, their job feels more like a prison. They are trapped by their need to provide an income. Many people don't really know what they want to do. Maybe they have felt that way for a long time, or maybe they are just starting out in their career and haven't yet decided what to do.

This book is written to help you move ahead in your career and discover what it feels like to be free and living with a career that is "on purpose". It is possible that, as you go through the Career Acceleration Process, you will realize that you have a specific calling to a certain type of career, in which case you are in for an exciting ride. But don't fret; you don't need a particular calling to achieve your full potential.

Your career success is not dependent on finding the perfect job. In fact, there is no such thing as a perfect job, and there is no such thing as a bad job. No particular job holds the key to your freedom or the bars to your prison. This is good news, because even if you have a job solely based on your need to provide an income and now feel trapped, you can still achieve the happiness and satisfaction that is your innate right.

The key to your career success and achieving your potential is in the way you fulfill your job, whatever job it is. If you feel good about yourself and your situation, you are more likely to be successful at what you are doing. The opposite is also true. In this book, we describe a process that you can apply to your abilities; one that will accelerate your career. And in doing so, you will fulfill your potential. It is a practical, progressive process that anyone can employ.

During their careers, David and Sharon have counselled thousands of people who have had workplace problems to deal with. What stands out about all complaints is this; the problem is almost always centred on someone else. It's my boss; it's my colleague; it's that customer, and so on. It is rare for someone to say, "I have a problem. I can't get on with my boss. Can you help me to understand my issue so that I can work with my boss better?"

To advance your career you must accept responsibility for your part in any relationship. Trying to resolve anything but your own issues is like adding bars to your cage. In this book, you will not find ways to deal with other people's problems. You will find plenty of ways to take responsibility for yourself, and by doing so you will be able to work productively with anyone. That is where success is found.

Your Career

When you look back on your life, you will probably see that your career path has meandered. However, it is probable that at certain times you took specific steps that propelled you to a new, higher level. It is possible that what you did to advance your career isn't obvious, or is veiled by a coinciding event that seems to be responsible for the change. Many people say that they happened to be in the right place at the right time. But that isn't the real reason why they moved up. If you knew with certainty which of your actions actually caused your progress, you might be able to replicate these actions and accelerate your career. With the awareness of the steps you need to take, you could reasonably expect to move ahead far more efficiently over the full span of your career.

Success doesn't happen by accident. You may benefit from a fortunate circumstance, but if you aren't ready to seize the opportunity, you will drop the ball and the opportunity will pass on to someone else who is ready. Reviewing the career path of any successful person will show particular points that were instrumental to their progress. We have plotted these key points and organized them into a practical Career Acceleration Process.

The encouraging truth is this: the steps to your career success are not particularly steep. What will set you apart from the majority of the work force is your willingness to apply yourself. If you are, we can assure you that you will be able to climb the steps. In this book, you will discover what the steps are and how to take them. You will then have a process that you can use to accelerate your career.

We have defined seven steps that you need to take in order to progress. At each step, there are multiple abilities that you need to be aware of, and working to develop. As you develop these abilities, you will assume increasing levels of responsibility. As your levels of responsibility increase, you will attract new opportunities. The exciting part of this process is that the time line for progress is up to you. You could go from an entry-level position to the boardroom in two years if you so desire.

The secret to accelerating your career and experiencing the satisfaction that comes with this acceleration is recognizing the abilities that need to be developed, and how to develop them. We have seen different people working at the same level, apparently with the same resources, but producing different results. On further examination, we noticed that the successful people had developed particular abilities. In most cases, the development of those abilities was random, and their advancement had depended on when a particular ability was developed. In addition, and of importance, their advancement was not because they applied for a more responsible job that happened to be available; opportunities for advancement came only after their abilities had been developed.

Career Blocks vs. Career Development

There are many reasons why people do not progress in their career as they would like. Most of the real reasons are camouflaged, so it is easy to focus on the wrong things. Sadly, in many cases people conjure up false excuses. This is fatal for their career dreams.

One obstacle that many people experience in their career is that they go through periods of development, and then stop progressing. Stopping the development process is not usually a conscious decision. Once we are comfortably settled into a position that we have been working to achieve, our attention gets distracted. For example, when we start in a new position, we are intense in our training efforts, and our abilities benefit from this process. We develop our abilities to a level necessary to function in the new position, but once we are competent, we become distracted or complacent, and our development process stops. This stop/start approach will stall your career.

Some people who don't reach their full potential blame external circumstances. The more likely cause is that they have not fully developed the required abilities. Most people don't get stuck because they're not capable of moving forward. They just do not recognize what needs to be done. They have stopped developing. They were not aware of the abilities necessary to take them to the next step. People can spin their wheels for their whole career, unaware that a few simple actions could release them from their frustration and propel them into a position that would be far more fulfilling and enjoyable.

Everyday distractions provide another obstacle. We all lead busy lives and for some people this means that they simply don't get around to doing the kinds of things that would accelerate their career. For some, this is not an excuse. Their lifestyle dictates their priorities, and career development occupies the importance they decide it should.

For others, lifestyle distractions are an excuse. In this case, moving forward requires honesty about how they spend their time. If you complain that you can't do what you need to move forward, for example, but you spend many hours each week on trivial activities, then it is time to be honest and decide how determined you are to accelerate your career.

The seniority of a person within an organization is not, of itself, confirmation that the person has developed the abilities needed. For example, a Senior VP may have under-developed communication abilities. You can be sure that whatever your own particular abilities gap is, it will cause anxiety for the people around you. It is not uncommon for people to rise to levels of responsibility without having developed all the required abilities. A key cause is that people are promoted based on their technical skill, while other abilities required to perform at higher levels are overlooked.

There is good reason to treat the service that you provide, and how it is developed, with as much importance as a company invests in the research and development of their products. To ignore product development would almost certainly be fatal to the business. A deliberate and meticulous process is defined to avoid the obstacles that might get in the way of product development and improvement. Usually, a senior person with a whole department is tasked with this critical function.

Much like the processes that are applied to developing and continuously revising a commercial product, your abilities should also follow a process to ensure that they remain relevant in the market. People who continuously develop their abilities are those who create higher value for their organizations, not only through their own direct efforts, but also because they inspire the people around them.

The Career Acceleration Process is designed to provide a development process that is equal to one that a business employs for its products. It will guide you toward the development of the specific abilities that will give you the best return for your efforts. When you have prioritized the abilities, and decided which of them you need to develop first, you can personalize your own career acceleration process.

To expand your knowledge about the Career Acceleration Process, watch this free video.
http://bit.ly/1ks11gn

The 7 Steps

What many people do not realize is that most of our actions occur while we are on automatic pilot. Many of our behaviours are learned in early childhood, and by the time we reach our productive years, this early conditioning significantly influences our productivity.

In order to advance in your career, you must recognize your pre-programmed conditioning. We call this Ground Zero. After acknowledging the impact of Ground Zero, you can realize your full potential.

The seven steps are divided into four stages.

DISCOVERY STAGE

In this stage, you become aware of who you are and what services you offer to others. This stage contains the first two steps of the Career Acceleration Process.

Step One—Functional: Identify your strengths and weaknesses and what career direction you want to take.

Step Two—Collaborative: Define what you have to offer to a business and how to work with other people.

DEVELOPMENT STAGE

In this stage, you go beyond the scope of your job and become more involved in business growth. This stage also contains two steps.

Step Three—Progressive: Learn what it takes to work effectively in a team environment and take on more responsibility.

Step Four—Constructive: Increase your influence on your business and expand the scope of the business.

DELIVERY STAGE

In the Delivery Stage, you become responsible for many people and the well-being of your organization, and climb two more steps.

Step Five—Leadership: Learn what is required to lead people and business.

Step Six—Executive: Discover what is required to provide strategic direction for an organization.

DESIGN STAGE

At this stage, you define the landscape for many and you have the potential to leave a lasting legacy. This stage contains the final step of the Career Acceleration Process.

Step Seven—Visionary: Realize a vision that will influence the lives of many people, and leave a legacy.

In most companies, positions that require a certain level of responsibility are offered to the people that have displayed a similar level of responsibility. Notice that "displayed" is in the past tense. It isn't typical for a person to be given a higher level job if they haven't already given a clear sign that they will perform well at that level. As you develop abilities that take you from one step to another, your levels of responsibility will increase and it is very likely that you will receive commensurate opportunities. At this point, you are in the driver's seat of your career, and you can choose how fast you want to accelerate, and how far you want to go.

Being aware of the abilities required to accelerate your career is a step in the right direction, but on its own, it is not enough. Applying what you learn is where the acceleration will occur. You will discover that there is no lack of opportunities for people who continually invest in their own development.

Through reading and understanding the material in this book, you will discover a progressive, practical process that you can learn, customize to your needs, and apply. We have sprinkled anecdotes throughout the book to help describe the abilities, and what you need to do to develop them. While the anecdotes are based on real experiences, the names and some details have been changed to protect the privacy of those involved.

GROUND ZERO
OBEDIENCE TO HUMAN MIDDLEWARE

At all levels of responsibility, and throughout our lives, we use our abilities to perform tasks. All of our abilities come wrapped in pre-programmed behaviours, which are very important to the way we complete our tasks. Since our style of behaviour occurs automatically, we call this "Auto-obedience". The automatic nature of this behaviour has a significant impact on how we perform and how much responsibility we take on. Our Auto-obedience emanates from what we call Human Middleware (HMw), and we will define what we mean by this a little later in this chapter.

In addition to Auto-obedience, there is also "Conscious Obedience". We display Conscious Obedience when we decide to be obedient to laws or procedures that benefit us. This is a decision we make with conscious thought; for example, to follow legal and social laws that make our environment safe and acceptable to inhabit. Working in a company requires obedience to job specifications. Being obedient to guidelines that are valuable to us, and to the organization or community that we are working with, is generally accepted as productive and beneficial.

Defining Human Middleware (HMw)

Middleware is a computer term that we use as a metaphor to explain where our behaviours are rooted. A computer system is made up of various levels. At the most basic level is hardware. The next level is the operating system; it is what provides functionality to the hardware. At the user level, we have applications. Applications enable the computer to perform specific tasks. Between the operating system and the application level is where we find middleware. Middleware is software that connects the two. Middleware is needed for the applications to function with the operating system.

Middleware is an important, yet largely invisible, level of the computer system.

If we apply computer terminology to humans, middleware is that part of our system that is responsible for our automatic actions. Our attitudes, skills, behaviours, and beliefs; in fact, all of our conditioning from prior years, is stored in our Human Middleware, our HMw. A lot of the programming is done at an early age. Indeed, it is possible that some key behaviours and reactions we display in the workplace are the results of how we interpreted experiences as a child. Our conditioning influences us daily, and will continue to do so into the future. It isn't difficult to imagine how relying on old programming of our HMw can keep us stuck in the past as we try to move forward. Equally, it is not hard to imagine how recognition and continual development of our HMw programming can be the source of high productivity and the fulfilment of our potential. Our HMw is continually evolving. At any time a pre-programmed condition can be overwritten by a more powerful experience that changes our programming for that condition.

In addition to the behaviours that emanate from our obedience to our HMw, there are also elements of our behaviour that have been programmed in our genetics. Our genetic abilities are subject to development, and are influenced by experiences stored in our HMw. For example, a person who is good at a sport, but is forced to play by an over-controlling parent, might associate unpleasant emotions with the sport. Even though there is a genetic ability to perform, obedience to the early programming of the HMw might suppress that ability, and in that case, the ability may never be developed to its full potential. As our HMw is subject to conditioning over the years, we could, quite literally, camouflage or bury deep beyond recall, our greatest abilities. It is even possible that due to our formative conditions, we might never have had the opportunity to discover our greatest abilities, let alone develop them. As the years roll forward, our abilities may remain dormant, hidden by all the distractions that come into our lives.

Apart from storing enormous volumes of data, the filtering of incoming information that our HMw provides is imperative to our ability to function. Not only does the HMw filter incoming information against huge volumes of data, it also refines the feedback so that we are not overwhelmed with possible responses. This is one reason why two perfectly rational people can have the same experience, but interpret it quite differently.

As we go through life, the volume of data stored in our HMw grows exponentially, and consequently our conscious activities are increasingly controlled by the programming and our obedience to it. We come to a point where most of our daily behaviours and decisions are run on cruise control or auto-pilot. To say that our HMw influences everything we do would not be an overstatement. Of particular importance: in some cases our filtering and refined feedback is beneficial, and sometimes it isn't.

Auto-Obedience

The programming of our HMw and our auto-obedience to it has a significant impact on our outlook and productivity. For example, people who have had painful experiences when making decisions, could go through their whole lives avoiding decisions. That could be the source of continued deflection of responsibility, and may be costing them opportunities that otherwise would have been possible. Alternatively, they may have had very positive experiences making decisions, and therefore, they feel very comfortable putting forward ideas and suggestions. To some managers, being able to make decisions might be regarded as a sign of confidence, or even higher intelligence, and people exhibiting this ability might be more likely to be given additional responsibilities as a result.

There are many real world examples of how auto-obedience emanating from HMw influences our productivity in a positive or negative way. Understanding this process is extremely important.

Even if you have not yet been consciously aware of how auto-obedience affects your behaviour, we can assure you that it already has had a significant positive or negative impact on your career.

Let us illustrate this process with two anecdotes based on real situations.

Andrew and Joe got into an argument at a meeting. Andrew said something about the way the office was being run. The way Joe's HMw filtered Andrew's comments put Joe on the defensive, and he immediately responded critically. Joe's HMw was influenced not only by what Andrew said, but also by the tone in which he said it. The conversation became confrontational, and the outcome was not favourable for either of them.

It is possible that even as Joe responded, he was aware that he was on the defensive, a condition rooted in his HMw. But it was too late; Joe had staked his claim and now felt the need to defend his response and back up his aggressive tone. Even if what Andrew said was inaccurate and offensive, Joe's response, driven by auto-obedience to his HMw, gave him no chance to use his ability to handle this confrontational situation. Had he taken a moment to recognize the signals that he was about to react from auto-obedience, he could have taken a moment to control his response.

We usually get a sign: an increase in energy, a flush, or a flutter, for example, when our auto-obedience has been engaged. Recognizing the signs is an important step in developing your ability to handle difficult situations in a controlled manner, and will also serve to advise your HMw that reprogramming is required. If you take a moment to recognize the programmed reaction, the next time you face a similar situation, you can adjust your reaction. If you repeatedly take time to reconsider a situation based on the signals that accompany obedience to your HMw, eventually your HMw will reprogram itself, and your automatic reaction will change accordingly.

Another illustration:

Martin was known by everyone to be very negative. He could always be counted on to sabotage meetings with his grouchy attitude. Others in the organization, therefore, regularly discounted his opinions. One day, in a coffee shop in the building where he worked, John overheard Martin complaining yet again. He was moaning about being tired from a late meeting the night before. The conversation also revealed that Martin was the president of a large national volunteer association. It seemed inconceivable that this negative person could hold a position of such high responsibility. When John asked what Martin did for their organization, he discovered that Martin was a specialist in the area that John needed information about.

John started using Martin as a resource and was amazed at the wealth of knowledge Martin had. Martin had been withholding information from everyone else because of his HMw programming, which was based on previous negative experiences. John's normal response would have been to avoid Martin. However, after John adjusted his responses, he was able to filter out Martin's negative comments and develop a very constructive and beneficial working relationship.

This example shows how understanding the process of obedience to the HMw can be beneficial, not only to your programming, but it can also help you to be productive with those who are being led astray by their own HMw programming.

Your HMw can direct you to behave in different ways, even for situations that seem similar. It is very common for a person to behave in a very favourable manner under one set of circumstances and in an unfavourable manner in another situation. A person isn't always "arrogant;" they behave in an arrogant way depending on the circumstances and their HMw programming. One can quite easily appear arrogant one moment, and then understanding the next.

This will generally lead to questions like, "Why is he such a pain in the office, but easy to get along with at the social event?"

This dichotomy is proof that we all have the ability to act in one manner or another, and at some level we choose what our behaviour will be. This further confirms that being aware of what programming we have accepted becomes pivotal to reaching our potential.

Recognizing Obedience to HMw in Others

As John demonstrated in the coffee shop with Martin, recognizing the behaviours that emanate from other people's HMw can be an ability that has powerful possibilities. It may be easier to recognize the HMw behaviours of others than it is to recognize your own.

You may not feel comfortable working with another person. Why is that? It might be that their auto-obedience is producing some sort of behaviour that is disruptive to you and many people around them. Identifying that they have problematic behaviours may give you some clues about how best to work with them in a productive manner.

Let us look at the example of a bullying boss. It's possible that the boss learned at some earlier point in his life that bullying was the way to get things accomplished. It became a pattern that is now deeply programmed into his HMw. If your boss is a bully, and you want to stay in your job, it would be beneficial to learn how to work with your boss. But how can you avoid being stressed by the bullying behaviour?

You may have tried various ways of dealing with your boss, without success. Understanding that you are not the source of the bullying is important. The key to making life more tolerable with your boss is disassociating the behaviour from the intent. This task is actually centred in your own HMw. We all have had to deal with bullying behaviour at some point in life, and our programmed response is typically aggressive or submissive, neither of which is productive. Surprisingly, you will find that even people who have strong negative behaviours emanating from their HMw often have commendable intentions. It is the way they deliver their message that has gone awry. If you are able to uncouple the bully's behaviour from his message, you might actually be able to benefit from his experience.

The following section describes more examples of counter-productive behaviours that you might have to deal with. Do not be surprised if you see some of these behaviours in yourself. Recognizing them is an important step in accelerating your career.

Arrogance: People who behave in an arrogant manner act as if they always know more than everyone else. This behaviour often comes from a feeling of insecurity. This is a defensive behaviour, and is a significant barrier to reaching one's potential. Arrogant people tend to think they know what is needed to take higher levels of responsibility, but many of the people around them see a different picture.

Workplace Fear: Workplace fear is linked to worrying about an undesired outcome; for example, fear of being wrong and having your actions exposed to the criticism of others. Fear produces a defensive behaviour and can come across as arrogance, or alternatively, as timidity and passivity.

Victim: Victims tend to think that the world is out to do them wrong. In the workplace, it is common for organizations to go through frequent transitions. If a person sees transitions as victimization of the staff, any form of change becomes a debilitating occurrence. A common trait of victim behaviour is blaming others for problems and difficulties.

Entitled: Entitlement is a behaviour that is displayed in people who are programmed to think that awards should be given to them as an obvious recognition of their personal rights. They believe that the policies of the company should be written to ensure they get what they want or need. Entitlement generally stems from irresponsibility, and the need to be cared for by others.

Passive-Aggressive: This behaviour occurs when people don't agree with some condition in their environment. People who display passive-aggressive behaviours are those who can't accept this condition, and are unable or unwilling to try to change it, but have decided to stay in the environment. Because they are unable to accept or change the condition, they complain about it frequently and try, in disguised ways, to sabotage the condition or the person who created the condition.

As you read through this book, you will discover the many consequences that auto-obedience has on your career and what you need to do to ensure that you perform at your highest level.

Our purpose for writing this book is to provide a process for recognizing and developing your capabilities to allow you to perform at your own highest level of responsibility. The HMw has an enormous influence on whether and how you reach your highest level of responsibility. It is programmed over many years and can be reprogrammed for the areas that are not supporting your best interests. This re-programming is a key step to moving forward. Equally important is being able to recognize and detach the negative behaviours of others from the individual, in any given situation. Being able to work beyond the negative behaviours of others is an ability that will give you a major advantage in performing to your highest potential.

The first step in reprogramming your HMw is identifying the behaviours that you display under specific conditions. As we identify the abilities that we all develop as we go through life, you will see how the behaviours that are programmed into your HMw have a substantial effect on your performance. Behaviours can be changed, and the success you can achieve in your working life can be significantly improved.

 To expand your knowledge about Ground Zero, see this free video.
http://bit.ly/1fCBlpT

Stage One

Discovery

Your career will follow four distinct stages. In the Discovery Stage, you become aware of who you are and what service you can offer. You will learn how to work with other people.

This stage contains the first two steps of the Career Acceleration Process.

Step 1: Functional—Learning about Yourself

Step 2: Collaborative—Working with Others

Functional

INTRODUCTION

At the Functional step, you will evaluate yourself and become aware of your natural tendencies. You define your skills, and using them as a guide coupled with your interests, set a general course on which to travel. The age-old question: "What will I do when I grow up?" is not one reserved for young people; there are many people who have reached middle age who still ask that same question.

By contemplating the abilities outlined in this first chapter, you will gain a significant advantage in answering your question. From the moment you decide to get serious about what you want to accomplish in your career, development of the abilities in this section will become easy for you, and you will become impatient with excitement at the prospect of what they can do for you.

We have divided the Functional step into two sections. The first section is My Attributes. The abilities described in My Attributes are about discovering who you are and what you are capable of doing. The second section is called Powering Up. The abilities in Powering Up are all about how you project yourself and your service to others. You will quickly discover as you navigate through your career, that what you can do and how you are perceived by others has an enormous effect on your personal success.

We will introduce Powering Up in more detail after we have covered My Attributes.

MY ATTRIBUTES

Having an honest and comprehensive understanding of what makes you tick is vital to your success. If you cheat yourself by either over-inflating your abilities, or blaming others for your situation, and decide that you cannot change, you will have to settle for a level of responsibility in your career far below that which you may have otherwise achieved. Likewise, if you under-value your abilities for reasons such as modesty or self-doubt, you may have to settle for a responsibility level far below that which you could have achieved. It can be very frustrating for others to see that you are capable of doing so much more, but you don't see that for yourself.

My Attributes is about you, and it requires you to be honest with yourself. Everything you build from this level forward will depend on the sincerity and completeness of the work you do in My Attributes. It is the foundation on which your career will be built.

The great news about the construction of your personal foundation is that you can continually work on it, and in fact, you should continually work on it!

You will change over the years and many of the abilities that you define today will change over time. This means that whatever your stage currently—whether you are an executive or just starting out—evaluating your abilities in My Attributes is relevant. There is an important discovery that you will come to as we cover the abilities in all the levels. When your transition from one level of responsibility to another is blocked, often it is not because of an ability associated with your current level but rather with an ability that was not developed at a previous level.

We sincerely wish you well in working through this book. It is our intent to provide you with a process that will have a stunning impact on your career.

Take the first step to fulfill your career potential.

Unravel Yourself

In order to unravel yourself, you need to take a comprehensive look at how you behave under various conditions. You need to recognize areas of strength and weakness and focus on the areas that seem incongruent with your basic principles and values.

When you are not consciously developing your capabilities, you operate at a lower level. You have numerous skills that are stored in your HMw. You learned some of these skills without being consciously aware of doing so. As an example, when you watch the news on television, you will see a story about a dramatic event, and you may be unaware that you are also learning about peripheral subjects such as the history and geography of the region in which the story is taking place.

Most people spend their lives utilizing partially developed or unrefined capabilities. Unfortunately, most people are unaware of this fact, and travel through life under-achieving and not realizing their potential. By the time they enter adulthood, they have developed some capabilities, but rarely are they functioning at full capacity in all areas. Most people are barely scratching the surface with most of their capabilities. This presents a wonderful and practical opportunity for growth. The question is: how to do that?

Here is the answer.

Spend time thinking about yourself. Most people are so busy that putting aside ten to fifteen minutes a day to simply think about themselves is a tall order. To find the time, consider that there are multiple activities that you do during the day that do not require conscious awareness and these times can be used for this exercise; for example, taking a shower or a bath, driving, and any number of activities that you do habitually and which don't require conscious thought.

The process of unravelling yourself using self-directed thoughts is not a quick fix process. However, the good news is that if you set aside ten to fifteen minutes per day, within three or four days, you will begin to see a pattern in your thoughts, and you will have begun a journey that will be broad and as deep as you choose to make it.

There is a famous Buddhist proverb: "When the student is ready, the teacher will appear." As you define your line of thought around your experiences, skill sets, hopes, and desires, as if by magic, your picture of yourself will begin to materialize. You need to be open to seeing signs. They could appear at the grocery store, or from something a child says to you. Insights can come in any number of different forms, but once you start the process of thinking about yourself, these messages will arrive.

As you continue a regular practice of self-consideration, you will be astonished with how much you know about yourself, but that you have not been conscious of. This knowledge will play a key role in the development of your capabilities and fulfilling your potential.

What you may find intriguing as you go through this process, is that once you become conscious of the development process, you will find that you use certain skills at work that you don't use at home, and vice versa. When you start to understand that we don't lead parallel lives, you realize that you cannot be successful in one aspect of your life without being successful in the other. So, developing your capabilities for one area of your life benefits all areas.

After you have started the practice of self-contemplation, the process will progress quite naturally.

Set Your Compass

The next step is to clarify what is important to you. We need to be consciously aware of our values and principles.

By values, we mean having a list of the things that are really important to you in life, and prioritizing them. To help define your priorities, consider the situation in which your child is sick, and you also have an important project at work. Which one takes priority—staying home with your child, or going to work to complete the project?

There is, of course, no black and white. It is rarely either/or. So we apply a grading to our values. Below is a sample list of values. These are listed to serve only as a definition of what a value is. This example list is not intended to be your value list. Take the time to create your own prioritized list.

Sample Personal Values List (in no particular priority)

- ◊ community involvement
- ◊ education
- ◊ family
- ◊ financial security
- ◊ good health

If values define what is important to us, principles describe the way we behave toward our values. Our principles influence the way we act.

As you have just done for defining your values, you also need to do to define your principles.

Here is a sample list of what a person might define as their principles.

Sample Personal Principles List (in no particular priority)

- ◊ honesty
- ◊ integrity
- ◊ loyalty
- ◊ fairness
- ◊ respect

As an example, consider the case of a cashier giving you too much change after a purchase. If honesty is one of your key principles, then you would probably return the money. If accumulating money is a value, and honesty is not one of your principles, you might keep the extra change.

Your values and your principles play a key role in your behaviour and your decisions. There are circumstances that you will be exposed to that will highlight your principles, and how you apply them, based on the situation. You may become aware of your values and principles as the result of a random occurrence during your normal daily activities. For example, if you drive past a wounded animal on the road, would you stop or would you continue? If one of your top values is tending to vulnerable animals, then you are likely to stop. If it isn't, then you would carry on.

There is no judgement in this—we are not saying that one value is nobler than another. And there are circumstances where, on a regular basis, we are required to follow the values and principles of a third party, for example the values and principles of your work-place. This will be discussed later.

Identify Your Purpose

What is your current purpose in life? What is it that drives you? If you look forward to the next five years, what would you like to achieve? If you look back on the last five years, what have you achieved? Are you happy with what you see? If you are not, it is likely because you did not have a driving purpose. If you do not set a driving purpose for the next five years, chances are that you will be in the same position then as you are now.

We are not talking about having a large house in the suburbs with two cars and a sailboat. Many of us get caught up in the day-to-day, and we feel as if life is about pleasing bosses or spouses, or making ends meet or buying that next bigger or better "whatever". Life is about more than acquisitions.

> *"Don't work in the dark, flood your career with light."*

A complaint we hear time and again is that people feel under-valued, and unappreciated, and that they are called upon to use only a fraction of what they feel capable of. They lament that their talents are going unused.

So where does this lament come from? From a desire to do more, to make a difference, to go home at the end of a workday feeling that their day on the job not only earned them money, but also made some small difference. People do not want to end their work-day feeling that, if they were to drop dead that night, no one would notice. What this tells us is that people need a central purpose to guide their lives. They need to know what they are here for so they have a yardstick against which to measure their accomplishments.

If we spend our lives trying to meet others' expectations, we will be miserable. Living our lives for others is like trying to catch waves upon the sand. People's needs and expectations are constantly changing. Since we are not telepathic, it is virtually impossible to remain continuously synchronized with someone else's thoughts.

We need to know our own thoughts, and what drives us.

To clarify your life's purpose, ask yourself three questions:

What am I good at?

What do I love?

What does the world need?

Mary was struggling with these questions, so she started by making a list of all the things she was good at. Her list included singing, performing, playing guitar, entertaining an audience, and teaching. She loved doing most of these things, but if she looked at how she spent her time, she never, ever took out her guitar just for fun. She only did it when asked to perform, and when she did, it felt like a chore. So Mary struck playing guitar off the list when she came to listing what she loved doing.

The last question, "What does the world need?" actually means, "What do my skills offer to others? What gives me satisfaction when working with other people?"

This is the key question, and Mary was able to answer it only by looking back at recent experiences. When she played guitar and sang in front of an audience, she had fun, but did not have any lasting sense of accomplishment. The satisfaction was fleeting. However, when she got up in front of an audience and taught them something, rather than singing a song, and she saw the lights in people's eyes as they learned something, her sense of satisfaction was much deeper. This tells Mary that her mission is about teaching people, and not about entertaining them.

Now it's your turn. Make a list of the things you are good at. Make a second list of things you love doing. Then reflect over the past few years of your life. What gave you the most satisfaction, and the greatest sense of accomplishment when using your talents with others? What led you to sense, at a deep level, that your contribution was valuable? After you have completed this exercise, you will know your purpose, be less affected by other people's opinions, and be better able to keep your life on track.

Know Your Natural Talents

To discover your purpose in life, you made a list of things you are good at. This gives you a list of your talents. These talents may be things that you do naturally because you were born with certain abilities, or they may be talents you developed because of a personal interest or external encouragement, perhaps resulting in your getting special training that developed them.

As an example, imagine that you were born with athletic ability, and that ability was fostered and developed through lessons, and by parents who were also athletic.

Now contrast this with the person who develops their natural athletic ability on their own, without parental influence or help, or the person whose athletic ability was never discovered at all.

The purpose of this section is to for you to become conscious of your talents. The earlier you become conscious of your talents, the more chance you will have to take full advantage of them. It is of utmost importance for you to think, on paper, of all the things that come naturally to you and interest you. Think outside of the box to come up with all of your talents. We want you to go beyond what you usually do for work or sport. You may think that planting a garden or painting are irrelevant, but they show talents for structure, order, and artistic presentation, for example.

Greatness comes from determining what you are talented in, and using your talents to the best of your ability. It will give you pleasure to invest your time in developing that talent, whether it involves taking a course, reading books, or talking with people who have accomplished similar things, and by asking them to become your mentors.

When you focus on doing what you are naturally talented in, you may be surprised that it causes other talents to come to the fore to support it, making you good in things you never thought you could do.

For example, Cynthia was not good at math. She hated math in high school, and barely graduated because of her poor marks in that one subject. On the other hand, Cynthia has an artist's eye and takes exquisite photographs, so her family encouraged her to study photography at college. One of her required courses was physics, which requires the use of mathematics. Much to her surprise and delight, Cynthia found that when the math was linked to something she liked—photography—she did well, surprising herself and her family with a final physics grade of 100%! Cynthia will never be a mathematician, but this example demonstrates how focusing on your talents can bring unexpected strengths to the fore.

Uncover what you are truly talented in, and become the absolute best you can possibly be in that. Only then can your star rise.

Recognize and Work with Your Imperfections

Nobody is perfect. Recognizing your imperfections means understanding the areas in which you need help. It is important to be able to put aside any false pride and look for the kernel of truth in what people offer you as feedback. If you are honest with yourself, you will probably admit that you had noticed these things yourself, but brushed them aside.

Getting feedback is even more helpful if these imperfections were unconscious, and you weren't at all aware of them. In accepting this feedback, think about how valuable this new awareness will be to your future, and be grateful when the people around you have the courage to point out these imperfections.

It is important to note that we are not telling you to focus on and build up the areas in which you are not talented. Quite the contrary. While working in the areas in which you are talented, you may also have imperfections that are preventing you from achieving your full potential. If you are noticing these issues, or if people are pointing them out to you, it is important to pay attention.

Different people react differently to criticism, and some are better at receiving it than others. When people hear something about themselves for the first time, it may jolt them a little and hurt their feelings, or they might brush it off. But when they hear difficult things about themselves three or four times, they may get angry and say to themselves, "What is wrong with these people? Do they not see that I am doing my best?"

If this is you, put your anger in your pocket, listen, and do something about this feedback. If you hear the same criticism three or four times, it is imperative that you not blame the speakers. It is unlikely that they are all mistaken.

Beverly is a perfect example of how being unwilling to correct your imperfections can get you in trouble. Beverly landed a great new job working for a terrific boss. On her first day of work, however, she discovered that the new boss had been transferred, and because of a miscommunication, no one knew she was expected or what to do with her. To the department's credit, they sorted this out quite quickly, but Beverly had trouble hiding her disappointment. The new boss was not the mentor she had counted on, and Beverly very quickly noticed that her new boss found Beverly somewhat intimidating. Beverly did not care, really; she was proud of her abilities, and perhaps a little arrogant, and she thought that, if she did a great job, she would succeed anyway. Beverly was right in one way, but very wrong in another. She did, indeed, do very well in the special project to which she was assigned, but her arrogance alienated others and further intimidated her boss. Called into her boss's office one day, Beverly was expecting a promotion. She had done a fantastic job, all by herself, on a very complicated, national project which had an extremely short timeline. To her utter shock, she was fired! She had lost her job, simply for not listening. People had told her they found her arrogant and intimidating, and she knew it herself. What a loss—to her personal success, to her department, to the organization, and to their clients.

It is critical to recognize and work with your imperfections, whether they are pointed out by others or whether you notice them yourself. Do not expect yourself to be perfect. Having imperfections is normal, whether they are in behaviour, skills, or specific abilities. There may be one behaviour or inability that is preventing you from fully using your talents, and making a valuable contribution in your organization.

People have strange reactions to the discovery that they have gaps in their abilities. If you were playing tennis and noticed that you needed to work on your backhand, would you not work to improve it, whether it meant taking a lesson, increasing your practice time or both? Yet, when we notice imperfections in our behaviour, we often resist. The Career Acceleration Process invites you to recognize and work to improve any imperfections, so that you can be your best self.

People who have developed their capability to recognize and work with their imperfections also recognize that others are not perfect. They are able to accept other people as they are. They are sociable and non-judgemental, and they avoid being pompous or bigoted.

Know Your Stressors and Manage Your Reactions

When you squeeze a fruit, what comes out is fruit juice. When you squeeze or stress a human, what comes out varies, but is very telling. We all react differently under stress, and our individual reactions can vary with different types of stress. It is critical that you understand how you react to the stressors you may experience, so that you can use your positive reactions to your advantage and manage your challenging reactions.

Some people are natural emergency responders. When something urgent comes up, they jump right in and take control. It may not matter whether it

"Stay calm under pressure and turn a problem into an opportunity."

is a crisis with a project involving a valued client, a colleague having a heart attack, or a fire in the staff kitchen. Their emergency response clicks in, and they know what to do. They are organized and efficient under fire. We know whether we are one of these emergency responders, and who in the office has this capacity.

The emergency response is an example of a valuable reaction under stress. The situation may not have to be very serious. Some people just work better under deadlines. If you are the kind of person that responds well to stress or works better under pressure, it is important that your colleagues know this, and also that you set your work schedule to take advantage of this. One caveat, however, is that those who work better under stress can become procrastinators. It is never better to wait for things to become urgent before attacking them. It is far more advantageous to you, your colleagues, and your organization, to deal with things when they are important, thus leaving time available for fire-fighting only when necessary.

If you work less efficiently in an emergency, you need to know this and manage it. The first step is to know what your usual reactions are in different stressful situations. Take some time and look back over the past few years of your life. You may know that you do not like to be stressed, but if you do not take the time to plan, and you run on automatic pilot, you may be taken by surprise, and your negative reactions could damage your career. People have long memories for negative reactions they see in others.

What are your standard responses to stress in the workplace? How do you deal with that unexpected extra project, earlier deadlines, and enhanced specifications; with difficult colleagues, new directions, and new leadership? Do you panic? Do you withdraw? Do you get angry? Do you become ill?

Reactions can happen on mental, emotional, physical, and even existential levels. Here are some examples. Mentally, one can become confused, disorganized, and unable to concentrate. Emotionally, a person can feel, among other things, angry, sad, fearful, or insecure. Physical responses can include extremes such as overeating or loss of appetite, inability to sleep or sleeping too much, catching a cold or flu, and in some cases even high blood pressure or cardiac arrhythmia. Existential responses can lead you to ask, "What's it all for anyway?" or "Why do I care?" These can lead a person to becoming passive-aggressive and even depressed.

There will always be stressors at work that are out of your control. From your perspective, they may not even seem to make sense. Not having a periscope into the upstairs offices, you may not realize that these changes might be necessary, or even in the organization's best interests. You may not be able to control what happens in your organization, but you absolutely can, and should, control your response.

When you get squeezed, what comes out? Is your juice sweet or sour? If it is likely to be sour in certain situations, don't let yourself be caught by surprise. Take the time to plan how you will manage any less-than-positive reactions, and keep yourself moving forward.

Have a Sense of Humour and
Don't Take Yourself too Seriously

One of the more stressful types of behaviour to deal with in the workplace is exhibited by those who take themselves, or their work, too seriously. You may make a simple comment, intending no harm, and they jump down your throat, as if your remark were directed at them personally. People need to be able to take themselves lightly at work, and not look for criticism and negative intentions in every comment. Over-sensitivity will invariably get you into trouble. We are not advising you to disregard the potential seriousness of others' comments, nor are we saying that you should be flippant in your attitudes or careless in your work. Quite the contrary, we encourage excellence in managing yourself, your relationships, and your responsibilities. In having a sense of humour, we encourage the ability to laugh lightly at yourself, your own foibles, and the foibles of others. We also encourage you to develop the ability to brush off non-helpful criticism.

To be successful in the workplace, and to take on increasing responsibility, thereby making greater contributions, one has to be able to listen to others, and acknowledge when other ideas or ways of doing things are better than ours. If we cannot do that, we will never grow, either personally or professionally. If someone comments on your work and you jump down their throat, two things will happen. First, they will think that, in addition to the problem they perceive in your work, you have an attitude problem. Second, they will hold back from offering future comments, not wanting to trigger a bad reaction from you. Reacting defensively is not helpful to anyone. When someone points out that you have made an error, and you discover that they are correct, the best way to diffuse the situation is to acknowledge the error, thank the person, give them a big smile, and perhaps add a humorous self-directed remark.

If someone offers you criticism or suggestions that you believe are either unnecessary or incorrect, it is essential that you find a way to acknowledge and deflect the criticism. Your wisest choice is to display a sense of humour, but without denigrating the person who is offering the criticism. This can be particularly challenging if the other person speaks to you in an arrogant or demeaning tone. It is important to be able to lighten up the situation without succumbing to sarcasm.

If you notice that someone else has made an error, using humour is tricky. They did not make this error on purpose, and would probably welcome your intervention, if done in the correct way. Done incorrectly, by making the individual the object of your humour may be funny once, twice, or even three times. But humour that puts others down will eventually backfire on you, and you could find yourself in the Human Resources office, facing a harassment complaint. Being able to use humour when others make errors, without criticizing the individuals themselves, is a fine art, and well worth practising and perfecting.

Workplace challenges such as reorganizations, new staff, new projects, changes in requirements, and errors can be stressful events. It is important to remember that, while these things are important, they are not life and death situations. If a colleague were to have a heart attack on the job, that's serious. If there were to be a fire or a terrorist threat in the building, that would be catastrophic. Put in context, reorganizations or changes in requirements are not high on the list of possible disasters. They may feel terribly threatening in the moment, but people who cannot take workplace challenges with a smile, and a "let's get it done" attitude, will not have the tenacity to survive organizational life very long. Organizations are replete with challenges that have to be faced on a daily basis. Being able to deal with these efficiently and positively, with a lightness of heart and mind, will make you easy to get along with and ensure that you experience a long, successful, and increasingly responsible corporate life.

MY ATTRIBUTES SUMMARY

Working on My Attributes involves discovering who you are and what you are capable of doing. Example attributes are listed below, followed by the key behaviour that characterizes each one. We have added the negative behaviour in the last column to help you recognize how people present themselves when that ability needs to be developed.

Use this chart as a handy reminder of what you need to accomplish and how you can stay on track to fulfill your career potential.

Abilities	Positive Behaviours	Negative Behaviours
Unravels self	Knows own skills and abilities, on solid ground	Self-critical, unkempt,fearful
Sets compass	Knows own values and principles	Lacks direction
Identifies purpose	Purposeful	Vacillates
Knows natural talents	Smart, clear thinker Builds on strengths	Expert at nothing
Recognizes and works with imperfections	Takes criticism well Always improving	Arrogant
Knows stressors and manages reactions	Cool under pressure	Prone to panic
Has a sense of humour	Easy to get along with Relaxed	Oversensitive

POWERING UP

In Powering Up, you will discover and develop your ability to project yourself and your service to others. Ultimately, you will progress from one level of responsibility to another, largely based on how other people perceive you and your services. While occupational skills can and do play a role in moving you from one level to another, skills alone will only take you so far. Determination and persistence, even when accompanied by disagreeable behaviours, can move you up the levels of responsibility. However, to provide a lasting and satisfying contribution for yourself and those around you, positive interactions with others will play a significant role in your progression.

People evaluate you based on their perceptions of you and your service. Because their perception is only their opinion, something over which you have no control, do not let another person's opinion restrain you from achieving your goals. Listen to opinions, analyze them, and then make your own conclusions based on your best interest.

How you behave around people significantly influences their opinion of you, if you are perceived in one way by people who know you well, and in another way by casual observers and acquaintances, you should recognize this as a red flag. Being consistent in your interactions is generally the sign of a solid foundation. Acting from your clearly defined and regularly recalled values and principles is the best way to be consistent. When you are consistent in your behaviour and reactions, most people will form a similar opinion of you, and they will have a solid basis on which to evaluate your capabilities, and how these capabilities can best be aligned with the organizational objectives.

Once you are presenting a consistent image, your next step is to provide your valuable service. While your primary urge is to provide for yourself, you will learn that focusing on how you project yourself to others will move you up the levels of responsibility very quickly. Ultimately, everything we do has a self-serving element, but even the most altruistic person cannot change the natural law of giving and receiving. It is simply impossible to give without receiving something in return, even if your sincerest desire was purely to give. Receiving doesn't necessarily have to be in the material sense; sometimes the satisfaction we receive is worth more than the cost of the service. We have all experienced the feeling of satisfaction we get when giving a gift to someone, and knowing that it was appreciated.

When you apply this simple law to your career, you will be astounded at how many opportunities appear, and how quickly. Providing your service in a way that is focused on helping others, even when you are not being paid directly will facilitate your progression from one level to another at warp speed. Prepare to go to infinity and beyond!

Transitional

The transitional ability involves understanding your organization and how you fit in. You have taken the time to identify your values, principles, skills, and abilities. You have set your compass, and identified your purpose. You know your natural talents, and you are willing to minimize the effects of your imperfections and stressors. You are on the lookout for instances in which you are acting from auto-obedience, you are tolerant of others, and you know that you are valuable to the organization.

Now you are ready to look for opportunities for growth, and achievement of your purpose within your organization.

First, take a comprehensive look at your organization. Start with where you are now. What are the values and principles of those around you? What is important to them? What is important to your boss?

Next, branch out to the parallel areas in your organization. Who works in these parallel areas, and what are their skills and abilities? What are their values and principles?

Third, move up the line. Look at your boss's boss, and at his or her colleagues. Understand what is important to them and how that fits with what is important to you.

Finally, reach up and try to understand the mindset of the leaders of organization. What are their strengths? What is important to them? Who among them would be good role models?

In most cases, people get a job, and then they get busy in their own cubicle doing their own work. Many soon get caught up in day-to-day routines, and the next thing they know they are 55 years old, looking toward retirement, and realize that they have not fulfilled their expectations.

You will not be in this sad situation because you are now in possession of the career acceleration process outlined in this book. In this transitional stage, you are setting your course for success. Knowing the lay of the land prepares you to make course corrections along the way. Having a good understanding of the values, principles, and goals of your organization and the people around you is beneficial. Corporate knowledge enables you to chart a course that will maximize your productivity.

Manage Your Attitude

Think of a few different people you know at work. What are the first things that come to mind about them? You may be surprised to discover how strong and clear your impressions are. Perhaps you experience one of them as independent and confident, and another as insecure. Perhaps you see one as hardworking and trustworthy, and another as sickly and complaining. Their attitude, that is, the outward expression of their personality, is as obvious as a tattoo on their forehead.

People do not realize the extent to which they can control how they are perceived. This, in turn, dictates how they are treated.

Consider this example. Two women of similar age attended a seminar. Their feelings about themselves, and about the world around them, was reflected in their hairstyles and dress. One had long, blond hair and wore flashy jewellery, a sleeveless summer top, a short skirt, and sandals. The other had her long hair pinned up and wore a conservative pant suit with fashionable, understated jewellery. The instructor asked the class to guess what the two women did for a living. In stereotypical fashion, the class guessed that the blonde woman worked in administrative support and the other in management. They were shocked to learn that it was the other way around.

This was a stunning realization for the blonde woman, whose main reason for taking the course had been to learn how to gain respect from those over whom she had authority. She had entered the course complaining that people treated her as if she were a teenager; yet she had resisted changing her style of dress because she believed strongly that she had the right to wear what she wanted. It was true that she had the right to dress as she wished, but now she realized that her chosen style of dress was negatively affecting her career. She decided to change her attitude and came in the next day dressed entirely differently. She came in with her hair pinned up, and wearing a skirt and matching jacket. In addition, she carried herself differently, projecting an air of authority.

Your attitude toward yourself, toward your work, and toward those around you is defined when you wake up in the morning. Be aware that you decide how to present yourself. When people see you, they label you, and they treat you accordingly. If you want to be perceived differently, look at how you present yourself. If you want people to see you in a positive, professional light, make sure that your outward appearance projects that. Dress and carry yourself accordingly.

If you are going through a difficult period in your life, your attitude may be affected. If this is the case, it is important to separate what is work-related from what is not. If there are work issues that need correcting, take action rather than complaining. If it is home problems or health issues that are worrying you, seek help outside of work to get them resolved. Don't assume that people at work want to know your personal problems. They have their own challenges.

If you come to work with a great attitude, you will be perceived as someone with whom people want to spend time, and to have on their team. It will serve you well as you proceed in your professional development.

Be Grateful

It is important to continually remind yourself of what you have to be grateful for. Experiencing gratitude changes the way you look at things, giving you a more positive perspective. When we coach people who are unhappy in their work life, the first thing we often notice is that they are caught up in their day-to-day existence, and they are consumed by everything that is going wrong. Our first task is to guide them to be more aware of all that is going on around them, including what is going right.

In difficult times, it may be challenging to find something to be grateful for, but in our experience, feeling grateful can provide light in the darkness. There is magic in the ability to feel gratitude. It shifts the focus from the negative to the positive, and enables you to carry on. Rainy weather may spoil your picnic, but it is good for the plants. New software may be challenging to learn, but it will help you do your job better. Organizational changes can be disruptive, but usually lead to higher efficiency.

When you rise each morning, and before you go to sleep each night, take a few minutes to scan your personal and professional life and find a few things to be grateful for. Your day may include challenges and problems to solve, and we are not suggesting that you sweep these under the carpet and pretend they are not there. Attacking problems with an optimistic frame of mind, an attitude of gratitude for the parts that are working right, shines a flashlight on the difficult parts and makes them both easier to see and easier to solve. A positive attitude also makes you a more agreeable person—someone others will want on their team.

The ability to experience gratitude by continually reminding yourself of what you have to be grateful for is a strong basis on which to build a successful, progressively more responsible career.

Set Goals

In his book *What They Don't Teach You at Harvard Business School*, Mark H. McCormack describes a study that was conducted on students in a Harvard MBA program. The participants in the study were asked the following question, "Have you set clear, written goals for your future and made plans to accomplish them?"

It is fascinating to note that only three percent of the graduates had written goals and plans; thirteen percent had goals, but they were not in writing; and a staggering 84 percent had no specific goals at all. Ten years later, the same people were interviewed again, with interesting results. The thirteen percent of the class who had goals had average earnings that were twice as high as the 84 percent who had no goals at all. The three percent who had clear, written goals had average earnings that were ten times higher than the earnings of the other 97 percent. This study clearly underscores the value of setting goals.

Too many people run their professional lives by allowing others to set goals for them. What a pity it is to fail to achieve what you could have, if only you had aimed for it. Having goals and plans to achieve them are critical to your success.

In our experience, people who have clear goals succeed because they take responsibility. They see themselves as directors of their own careers rather than victims of circumstances. They are unlike most people, who accept a job in an organization and hand over control of their career in the process, checking their enthusiasm at the door when they scan their ID card. Victims blame "management" or "the organization" if things do not go the way they want, as if these two were actual entities, rather than simply collections of human beings with goals of their own. If your happiness and success depend entirely on the will and actions of others, you are aiming at an ever-moving target and can never reach your full potential. You need a personal yardstick against which to measure your success.

Setting goals puts you in the driver's seat of your life. Then, when opportunities come your way, you are in a position to benefit from these in ways that further your goals. For example, if you are very clear that one of your goals is to work internationally, you will have your eyes and ears open for any such opportunities that may come up in your organization. Even if the job requires learning a new skill set, you will do what you need to do to ensure that you qualify to be considered for that opportunity. And if you don't get that assignment, you will apply for the next one, because you are clear on what you want. Conversely, without goals, opportunities could be staring you in the face, and you wouldn't see them.

Having goals ensures some success, but having written plans to achieve your goals will produce astounding results. For example, it is easy for people to say they want to be millionaires, but the next time you hear that, ask them how they intend to accomplish their goal.

Paul had a goal to become a millionaire and here is how he achieved it. When he was asked how he was going to achieve his goal, he was able to describe his plan in detail. He was investing in real estate. He had acquired numerous rental properties and was currently seeking more. He was not only determined, but also on track, to achieve his financial goals. Three years later, his plan came to fruition.

The story of Paul's success leads us to our next point. Mapping out a plan to achieve your goals not only enables you to measure your success, it also alerts you to adjust your course if necessary.

You are responsible for your current career situation. If you are not where you want to be, you have the power to change it. To rise in levels of responsibility in your organization, emulate the three percent of students in the Harvard University study (who did ten times better than the other 97%). Set your goals and ensure that they are clear and measurable.

This will ensure that you know whether you are on track, when you need to adjust your map, and when you have achieved your goals. Then you will be in control of your own success.

For a success tool to help you set your goals, watch this free video.
http://bit.ly/1kLRDln

Use Affirmations

It is powerful to reaffirm daily what is important to you; to say or write your goals repeatedly, in the present tense, as if they were already accomplished. The Webster's Dictionary defines affirmation as: "A statement asserting the existence or the truth of something".

You may be wondering: if something has not yet happened, but we want it to, why would we say it had? To understand the answer to that question, let's look deeper.

We do not need experts in meditation to tell us that our minds chatter. We all talk to ourselves all the time. But eighty percent of self-talk is negative, and that self-talk has power. Is our negative self-talk the result of failing, or is failing the result of negative self-talk? Which came first? For decades, experts in meditation, psychology, quantum physics, business, sales, and self-help have been telling us that whether we say the words or just think them, we create our own individual truth. As Henry Ford said: "Whether you think you can, or you think you can't—you're right."

Positive affirmations have the power to change your thinking until your subconscious accepts the statement as true. Your new perspective alters everything you think, and affects all of your words, thoughts, and actions throughout your day.

Start by writing one or two affirmations. Examples might be: "I am in excellent health and full of positive energy", or "I surpass my sales targets by at least ten percent this quarter", or "My new venture is running smoothly and has a regular positive cash flow."

As you go through your day, notice your words, thoughts, and actions. Correct yourself when you notice any negative thoughts, and reaffirm your positive thoughts. Doing this will, in a very short time, alter what you think, see, and do. It will also move you in the direction of making your positive affirmations come true. It will help you to notice the things that are already there in your life to assist you, and, most important of all, it will convince your subconscious mind that you are ready and able to receive what you are asking for.

Know the Impact of Your Habits

In the section about Auto-obedience, we presented the concept of Human Middleware (HMw). We discussed both conscious and unconscious obedience, and how they can affect your daily working life. Habits are a dominant feature of auto-obedience. We all have habits, and we need them in order to function. If we had to think about everything we do, we could not get through the day. But to be effective, it is critical that you are aware of the consequences of your habits.

Here is an example of a habit and its possible outcomes. If you write texts or e-mails on your mobile device while walking down the hall, you are not aware of your surround-

"Don't do the same old things and expect something new."

ings, and you might miss opportunities. You might miss greeting an important client or a senior member of the organization who could contribute to your day.

Another common habit that people have is typing on their keyboard while participating in a teleconference. There are several potential consequences of this habit. You could miss important content, which could result in unclear deliverables and missed deadlines. Others listening to the conference call may hear your keystrokes, and assume that you are not listening. Perhaps there is someone important on the call; if that person finds your behaviour disrespectful, they may conclude that you are not professional, and ultimately contribute to stalling your career.

Take the time to become aware of your habits. Decide which of them are serving you well, and more importantly, which of them are not serving you well.

Having defined your habits and decided which of them are not serving you well, the next step is to change them. To change a habit, you must first be conscious of what constitutes a habit. A habit is formed when there is a need to regularly perform a task. By turning the task over to your HMw in the form of a habit, it frees up space in your conscious mind to focus on activities that require active thought.

Next, in forming a habit, you need the desire to perform the task. The desire will drive you to learn the ability to complete the task.

Finally, there must be a reward for completing the task. The reward might be the completion of a necessary function like brushing your teeth, or it might be work-related.

The reward might be an enjoyable experience like riding a bike, or the reward might be the avoidance of pain (getting run over by a vehicle), as with looking both ways before you cross the street. The more frequently a habit is performed, the more ingrained it becomes in your HMw.

To change a habit, you need to find the reward for the replacement habit. The habit you have chosen to change needs to provide you with an even better reward. Start by changing a simple habit and recognize the rewards you get; for example, wake up fifteen minutes earlier and read something relevant to your profession. Within a very short time (a few days, possibly), you will already be gaining new ideas that stimulate your thoughts.

After you have changed one habit, go on to another, and then another. Eventually you will form a habit of changing your habits. Here are a couple of examples of people who changed their habits and experienced very beneficial consequences. One person switched from music to talk radio during her morning drive to work and became considerably more knowledgeable and aware of current affairs. This new habit opened doors to more stimulating workplace conversations.

Another person developed the habit of listening to business books whenever he was in his car. This habit had a significant, positive effect on his career, because he had made learning a part of his day, every day.

In summary, it is imperative to be aware of the outcomes of your habits. Be conscious of whether your habits are working for or against you. Decide which habits no longer serve you, and commit to changing them. The right habits will produce the kind of results that you are looking for in your career.

To expand your knowledge about the impact of your habits, watch this free video.
http://bit.ly/1gAPYtP

Help Yourself First

In Steve's early days in medical school, he learned a valuable lesson on one of his first hospital rotations. He was admonished for racing to the bedside of a person who was experiencing a cardiac arrest. It would be a normal reaction to think that hospital staff should run when they hear the dreaded Code Blue called over the loudspeaker. The problem was that, when Steve arrived at the patient's bedside, he was so out of breath that he was useless on the resuscitating team. It is for this same reason that airline staff members announce, "Put on your own oxygen mask before assisting others." It would be a parent's natural reaction to assist their child before taking care of him or herself in an emergency, but that would be the wrong reaction. What good would they be to their child if they were to pass out?

It is in this context that we say: to help others, you need to help yourself first. Only when you are in top shape can you give your best.

Certainly you have heard colleagues complain that they cannot perform up to par because they are not feeling well, or something is going on at home, and on and on. It may sound harsh, but there is never an excuse to not perform well. If you are not well, take a sick day. There is no glory in saying, "I never took a sick day in my life", if there were days when you were grouchy or negative, or otherwise not performing as you should have been.

There will always be other things going on in your life, and some of these things may be serious. That is why it is crucial for you to ensure that you take care of yourself. See your doctor if the problem is physical. Talk to your psychologist, clergy, or close friends if the problem is emotional.

If you are lucky enough to have no personal or health issues, do your best to ensure that you stay that way. Eat well, exercise, manage your weight, and pay attention to your primary relationships. And if things do go wrong, your stamina and the strength of your relationships will help you to get through to the other side.

Put on your own mask first. Take care of yourself by keeping in top shape mentally and physically, and take the occasional sick day if required. If you ensure that you take care of yourself, you will be seen as someone who is reliable, who takes care of personal issues to ensure that they do not interfere with work, and who is capable of rising to higher levels of responsibility.

POWERING UP SUMMARY

The abilities discussed in the Powering Up section describe how to best project yourself and your service to others.

In the chart below, we have listed the abilities presented in this section, followed by the positive behaviours that characterize them, and the negative behaviours that show they are lacking.

Abilities	Positive Behaviours	Negative Behaviours
Transitional	Understands his or her fit in the organization	Works in own world
Has positive attitude	Confident, a pleasure to work with	Incongruent, negative
Grateful	Appreciative	Unhappy, focused on the negative
Sets goals	Responsible, has clear direction	Aimless
Uses affirmations	Has bright outlook	Relies on fate
Knows impact of habits	Tries and does different things, or does them differently	Stuck in old ways
Helps self first, to better help others	Reliable and healthy, mentally and physically	Unreliable, often sick or complaining

Collaborative

INTRODUCTION

Now that you have spent some time focusing on your abilities and how you fit into your organization, it is time to discuss the skills required for successful collaboration. The Collaborative step outlines the various abilities involved in working with others. As in the Functional step, the Collaborative step is split into two sections. The first section focuses on how others see you. How others perceive you is critical to your career success. In this section, we discuss the abilities that influence the opinions others have of you.

The second section is about how you work with others. In this section you will learn the various ways to communicate with others, and how to display the respect you have for their contributions.

INFLUENCING HOW OTHERS SEE YOU

When you focus your attention as much on how you do your job, as on what you do, you will have tapped into an important fact of working life. For many people, tasks become a routine part of what they do. After mastering their tasks, most people can generally run through their day on auto-pilot if they want to, but the part of the job that can make the difference between being stimulated and being bored is what happens between your tasks. When you lift your head from your desk, turn away from your screen, or put down your tools, there are a few moments that have an unconscious but influential impact on how you feel about your job. You may just gaze into the distance and think about something going on in your life. Or perhaps you share a few words with a colleague. You may over-hear a conversation. It is certain that you have a vivid sense of the work atmosphere. What you sense between tasks is as important as the quality of mortar between blocks in a wall. If the atmosphere is positive, the people around you are friendly, and the scene is appealing, you can quickly recharge and get on with the next task.

If you keep the importance of the time between tasks at the forefront of your mind, and ensure you contribute positively to the working atmosphere, your reputation will soar. We are not saying that you should become an office chatterbox, or the go-to guy for all the latest sports news. We aren't saying that you should walk about with a fixed, but clearly false, smile on your face, either. The most important thing is not to infect the environment with a negative attitude. Be positive, and others will think of you as good to have around. Then all you have to do is contribute occasionally with a friendly gesture, or question of interest to a colleague. Refrain from loud disagreements, and keep your opinions in check.

Conduct like this will ensure that you move from being good to have around, to indispensable.

Remember Why, Daily

Remind yourself, on a daily basis, what your current purpose is. This allows you to keep what you are striving to achieve at the forefront of your mind. People who have a purpose are perceived by others as confident and focused, and tend to display behaviours that inspire others. People who are focused on a mission tend to be more efficient with what they do, and they attract similar people. People want to work with them, and follow them. When we remind ourselves of our purpose, our passion is evident. Passion is a very positive and contagious behaviour. It shows that a person knows what they want and knows how to get it, and others will follow.

When you are clear about what you want, it has a positive effect on your behaviour, and can have a dramatic effect on your career.

When Daniel decided that he wanted to be a senior member of the sales team, he started doing things differently. He became more organized and more selective in what he did. He took a keen interest in learning about his profession, his business, and the industry in general. Over time, he noticed more people coming to him to ask for advice, even though he was not their direct supervisor. He got a reputation as a person who was going places, and people wanted to know how he did it. He gave presentations and informal speeches about his work habits. The driving force behind all of these positive changes was the fact that he kept his current purpose top of mind.

Know Your Brand

If you consider some of the larger companies and their products, what comes to mind? If you think about Mercedes, for example, you might think of high quality. If you think about Wal-Mart, you might think of a broad product offering, well-priced products, and stores everywhere. If you think about McDonalds, you might think of consistency and convenience. These companies and many others spend millions every year to ensure that their brand is clear and memorable. When we want to buy a product, usually we think; where can I buy it? If it's not an every-day product, who makes it, and do I trust them? Product manufacturers and suppliers want you to think of them first, so brand awareness is very important to them.

Now apply that reasoning to yourself. You have a product—your abilities and the way in which you apply your abilities. The important question in branding is: What do you want others to think about when they consider you?

Greg was a salesman in a large insurance company. He wasn't a top producer. He regularly made his targets, but that wasn't enough to get him noticed. Greg made a conscious decision that, if he couldn't move up the corporate ladder by productivity alone, he would create a brand for himself that would get him noticed. His business was a typical 9-5 business-to-business sales environment. There were about 20 sales people in his office and over 200 in the nation.

Greg created a brand to help him stand out. First he changed his arrival time to 8 am. He was now frequently the first person in the office each day. He also worked through until 6 pm and was often the last to leave the office.

As it happened, the building his office was in also housed the offices for the regional management team, and they had to walk through the sales area to get to their offices. Not coincidentally, the only other person in at 8 am was the regional manager, and it didn't take long for the regional manager to learn Greg's name, and he said, "Good morning", every day as he passed Greg's desk.

Then Greg upgraded his wardrobe. He bought a fine suit and shoes, and some new ties. He now looked the part of a successful sales person.

Next, Greg decided that he would use the extra hour in the morning and in the evening to read the newspaper and journals, looking for stories about his industry and particularly his customers. He also used this time to catch up on all his internal mail and corporate updates.

These changes significantly changed Greg's brand. He soon became seen as someone worthy of respect. He was now seen as serious about his business, and knowledgeable about what was going on in the industry, and within the company.

There's a strange twist to this story that Greg had not anticipated. His sales figures increased significantly. His presentations weren't noticeably different, his abilities hadn't improved overnight—at least he didn't think they had. Yet, by the end of the year he was in the top quartile of sales people in the country. His brand had become well known and Greg was set to move up.

Greg's story is not uncommon. If you look around your office with an eye to label your colleagues by brand, you will likely find one or two "Gregs", not just by what they wear or the office hours they keep, although these are good signs, but by the respect they command in the company, and so on. Defining a brand, marketing it, and living it are all vital in helping a business to penetrate the market. Brand development and awareness is no less vital for you.

> *"Project the image you want people to receive."*

Set Personal Targets

Let's face it, if the targets you set for yourself are significantly lower than what the company sets for you, it may be time for you to review whether you are applying your best abilities. Setting personal targets is all about being motivated, on a daily basis, to perform to your highest standard. If you are competent in your current role then, if you set personal targets that are realistic and you have assigned a personal meaning to them, it is likely that your targets will be at least in the same ballpark as the company targets, and probably higher.

Let's discuss company targets for a moment, because company targets could even be holding you back. Whether targets are based on who does what, and when, or they are production targets, like numbers of widgets produced or sales and profits, they are generally defined at a high level, and then averaged out over the staff. Some companies might weight their targets based on key variables such as seniority or prior performance, but in most cases, targets are assigned based on some logical equality.

What does that say? You are expected to perform at about the same level as everyone else in your company or your department. If you achieve that target, or even overachieve, you still may or may not be performing to your capability. How often do we all feel like we are really only performing well below our potential?

The problem is this: we humans have an annoying habit of relaxing after crossing the finish line, even if the finish line was set by someone else.

When we set our own targets, based on our own purpose and our own production needs, we cut ourselves loose from the restrictions and limitations set by the people who make the budgets. Even when our own targets are similar to the company targets, we feel differently about them because now we are achieving them with a personal purpose, rather than just meeting company targets.

David learned a very important lesson as he climbed the ranks in terms of sales productivity. He worked diligently to achieve the targets of the company, and through great efforts and good use of his abilities, he became the top sales person in his region. Being number one was a proud achievement for David, and over the next three years he worked hard to maintain his status. In fact one year he did so well, he was the number one sales person in the entire country. Then something changed. David's territory was shifted, and he lost a key customer. Soon he lost his title as number one in his region and he became bitter, not only about losing the top spot, but also towards the managers, and even the sales representative who gained by his loss.

Had David remained bitter, he would have missed an extremely valuable lesson, but he didn't. What David learned is that it was not wise to measure his abilities as the best sales person as judged by the company. This approach is ego-driven, and governed externally. He learned that it is much better to be the best sales person he could be, for the benefit of the company. This is service driven, and governed internally.

Once David understood this, his career took off in ways he never imagined possible. His goals were all inwardly driven, but this did not make him selfish. On the contrary, some of his goals were about helping others and the business to improve. David no longer saw his colleagues as competition. He took on more responsibility and helped the new sales reps. He gave regular presentations on sales skills, and showed how he had gone from being one of the pack to being consistently at or near the top. Once David started setting his own targets he was liberated from the limitations of budgets, and he went on to significant success in his career.

Setting your own productivity targets, in alignment with what you want to provide for yourself, your family, and your community, is necessary for you to fulfil your potential. Whether your targets are measured statistically, or based on the responsibility you take on, your goals are more important than anyone else's targets, and your chances of achieving them will be significantly better.

Take Action

Nothing gets done unless somebody does something. Inaction is a common cause of stagnation; your career needs continual action to keep it moving forward. It is easy to get overloaded with everything we have to do every day, so it is important to set time aside for the action required to move your career forward.

Your career and its progression are strongly influenced by cause and effect. Thoughts are the causes, and the effects of those thoughts must be your actions. Productive thoughts about identifying your current purpose, recognizing your abilities and how to market them, are key steps that will move you to reaching your highest performance level. Only by taking action on these thoughts will you bring them to life, along with the results you are striving to achieve.

Thoughts about the actions you can take are not gifts solely supplied to the rich, the educated, or the privileged. Look around you. How many well educated people seem to be under-utilized? How many wealthy or privileged people don't seem to be making much of a contribution to their community? That's not to discount the many rich, well-educated, and privileged people who do make wonderful contributions to society. The point is this: it's what you do, and not what you have, that is the common denominator of achievement.

Breaking your plans into bite-size pieces, and setting actions in motion for the small stuff is what will get you going. As Aristotle said, "Well begun is half done." When you are action oriented, you can't help but make progress in your career growth as a result.

Review and Improve

After you have recognized and defined your abilities, it is crucial that you continue to refine them. Most people inch forward in the development of their abilities by chance or by circumstance. If you look back to the beginning of your career, and you see no visible, dramatic change in your abilities since then, it is likely that you are growing by chance. Even under those conditions, you can probably list a number of skills that you use today that you did not have when you started, so imagine the influence on your career if you were to actively and consciously learn new abilities.

Lawrence joined a company in the shipping department. He was a conscientious person, and more than a match for his tasks. Lawrence also had a passion for Information Technology (IT), and he studied at every opportunity to learn the latest in that industry. Lawrence was also a good communicator, and he was able to help out on the IT side, providing information in easy-to-understand language to those who didn't speak HTML. After about a year in the shipping department, a position opened up in the systems division and Lawrence, although he didn't have the requisite formal qualifications, got the job. This was the start of a new career path for Lawrence. Today, while he has already moved several rungs up the corporate ladder, we know he hasn't reached the top of his own ladder yet, because he is continually reviewing and improving his abilities.

Stay Relevant

Beyond death and taxes, everything changes, and it can be scary just how quickly the changes occur. However, most changes are predictable if we watch for the signs. Even weather patterns are somewhat predictable, although we have little control over the influences that cause weather. In business, many changes to the economy, or product acceptance, or other agents of change, are the results of traceable causes. Of course, it's easier to see them in hindsight, but for most companies, the impact of market trends usually isn't seen overnight; most changes are subtle, and take time to filter through the system. This observation can also be applied to your career. Changes in management, or introductions of new products and services, are obvious signs that changes have been made and the effects will be rippling through to you soon.

When change happens, you can stick your head in the sand and hope it doesn't affect you. In truth, every change has some impact; this is most dangerous when it doesn't feel like any change actually occurred. The change may be noticeable, but so minor that you can carry on and ignore it.

The problem with ignoring change is that, by the time five or ten years have passed, the changes that you have ignored have accumulated, with you stuck firmly in the past, or living a life that seems to have gotten away from you. You may be wondering, "How on earth did I end up here?"

Imagine that you had decided not to join the communication technology revolution that has affected our lives so much in the office and at home. Even being a year behind the latest communications products can leave you without an opinion on some of the most talked about subjects, such as social network applications or the latest mobile devices. Being even a year behind on these changes would leave you seriously "out of the loop".

Change is a fact of life. If you embrace change, look for change, even be the agent of change, you will stay ahead of most other people in your field. Change keeps you stimulated, and accepting change as it comes can keep your career fresh and new, even if your title or position never changes.

Focus on Outcomes

There are countless examples throughout history of "mistakes" that help propel achievement. How many great advances have come out of the process of trial and error? Often, analysis of the failed experiment led to further research, which eventually resulted in discoveries even greater than originally anticipated.

The classification of something as right or wrong is generally based on the opinion of a person or a group of like-minded people. Certainly there are socially accepted conditions of right and wrong, as they relate to law and order, for example. But even within the generally accepted rules of the local culture, there is a wide degree of variance between what different people might call right or wrong.

We are not saying that, should something go horribly wrong (as compared to the objective), we might describe this as acceptable. But it is rare that outcomes are definitely right or definitely wrong. Applying the words "right" and "wrong", however, tends to put us in a particular mindset.

In one mindset, if a person doesn't perform the way you would like them to, you might label them as being incompetent, disobedient, or disagreeable to you. This could have a significant influence on your relations with that person.

In another mindset, if a project didn't work the way it was intended to, you might conclude that it's not worth continuing, and put it aside. The next time the project idea is raised, you will meet it with resistance because, "We tried that before, and it doesn't work."

The ability to assess an outcome objectively and without prior judgement is a skill that you need to develop. You must understand and consider the many elements to be taken into account, relative to the environment of the outcome, in order to learn from the experience. Making quick and thoughtless conclusions about whether an outcome is "wrong" will lead to detrimental programming of the experience in your HMw.

It takes a confident person to accept that a desired outcome has not been achieved, and after analysis, realizing that the outcome is the result, at least in part, of your own actions, suggestions, or information. But the confident person is also able to disassociate external occurrences with their self-worth, and can therefore review the situation objectively, and with a go-forward, productive mindset.

This confidence includes the ability to react with grace with those who blame you for making errors, because you recognize that they are stuck in a negative and unproductive mindset.

This does not mean that we abdicate accountability; quite the opposite. Those who can learn from their experiences will stand up and be counted when the responsibility is assigned. Those who can't accept their responsibility for the outcome are usually missing in action, or quick to provide reasons why they should not be held accountable.

Surely it is obvious, as you read this, which people are more likely to achieve higher levels of responsibility going forward. It is those who can objectively analyze outcomes, determine the next steps, and move on, who will continue to thrive in the organization.

Find the Challenge

A job is a job; its functions may or may not change noticeably over time. We cannot begin to count how many people we have spoken to, who complain about how dull their job is. One common reason for people leaving their jobs is that they no longer feel stimulated by their work. However, it is important to remember that a job is not designed to stimulate the workers who do it; it is designed to generate an outcome that will move the organizational objectives forward.

The real irony in this scenario is that those who leave a job because it is no longer stimulating often end up doing almost exactly the same job in another environment. The new environment stimulates them for a while, but that soon wears off. After a few moves, a person comes to the realization that, "This is it, and it doesn't get any better."

This worker then falls into a rut, and starts operating on auto-pilot, with the only blue sky on the horizon being retirement. With this mindset, time flies by, and the worker falls woefully short of achieving even a small percentage of his or her true potential.

The key to finding the challenge in what you do is to realize it is not what you do that will stimulate you, but what you think about what you do. Even if you start out by just acting as if you are stimulated, you will start noticing things that you can do, that were previously invisible to you. Most people have a fairly well-defined job description, but what else can you add to your tasks? Perhaps there is something additional you can do to break the monotony of the task. Providing that what you add doesn't interfere with the smooth running of the business, you are likely to gain appreciation from those who benefit from your additions. But you are not making these changes for others or for recognition—that will come at the Progressive step—you are doing it to help stimulate your own day.

Once you get into the habit of doing a bit extra or doing things a little differently every day, you will start experiencing a new attitude. No longer will you look at your job as a two-dimensional routine to be endured; you can now look at it as if it is an adventure. What can you find today that you can add your signature to? If you work seriously to develop this ability, you can transform the thoughts you have about your job, and will find yourself on the threshold of the next step up in your career acceleration process.

Taking control of your own enthusiasm is very important. Imagine the waste, realizing, after twenty or thirty years, that you are no further ahead than when you started out. The best time to begin accelerating your career is on your first day of work; the next best time is today. Find your challenge now!

INFLUENCING HOW OTHERS SEE YOU SUMMARY

Influencing how others see you is critical to your career success. In this section of the collaborative step, we have identified the abilities you can develop to present your services in a positive light.

The chart below highlights the abilities presented in this section and the positive behaviours associated with them. The negative behaviours in the right column are those that result from failing to develop these abilities.

Abilities	Positive Behaviours	Negative Behaviours
Remembers why, daily	Confident, focused	Unfocused
Knows own brand	Understands unique selling position	Goes around in circles
Sets personal targets	Competitive yet helpful, reaches beyond self	Use others to fulfil their needs
Takes action	Makes things happen	Stalls everything
Reviews and improves	Willing to try new things	Stuck in old ways
Stays relevant	Knows what's going on	Limited to own opinions
Focuses on outcomes	Learns from good and bad outcomes	Always right, even when they are not
Finds the challenge	Never seems bored, always energized	Always complaining about job, stagnant

How To Work With Others

Many of the difficulties that people experience when working with others are centred in their own perceptions, and actually have little to do with the other person. The opinions you have formed over the years, and which are stored in your HMw, play a significant role in how you interact with others. It is very important that you fully understand this, and take the time to identify what triggers you to be on the defensive or to go on to the offensive unnecessarily. There are, of course, people who are simply difficult to get along with. If you are able to create some form of productive relationship with this minority, it will certainly help you to move up the levels of responsibility quickly.

How you work with others is where the rubber hits the road. This involves both verbal and non-verbal communication. Verbal interaction covers speaking, reading, listening, anything that includes words and illustrations, in one form or another. Your choice of words is very important in your communication, as is your ability to listen.

What many people do not realize is that non-verbal messages are so strong that they can cancel out the words you say. If you ask someone, "Would you please close the door", but you use a harsh or sarcastic tone, the person will consider you rude. They will not even have heard the word "please". Non-verbal communication involves the unspoken messages that we receive and make judgments on, including our impression of how a person looks, acts, and performs. We even make judgements about what a person's intentions are, and we act as if that were their reality. We don't even check to find out if we are correct.

All methods of communication contribute to how we perceive others and how we are perceived by others. It is easy to understand how communication is a master skill for success.

Being a communicator doesn't mean having a natural ability to stand in front of a crowd and make a stunning presentation. Although that certainly helps, it is not required. We know many fine leaders who are not great speakers. As with most abilities, just being aware of what to avoid and focusing on a few relatively easy skills, will put you ahead of the crowd. As you demonstrate the confidence that comes from mastering these skills, opportunities will be presented to you.

Master Your Communication Skills

A key ability in collaborating with others is, of course, communication. Many people think that communication is about telling someone something; what they think, what they believe, or very often, what they want the other person to do. They can be surprised if the other person does not seem to understand, or doesn't do what they are told to do. The key here is that communication is not about telling, it is about mutual understanding. Communication is a two-way street. The word "communication" is actually from the Latin word, "communicare" (pronounced com-mu-ni-ca-ray), which means to impart, share, or make common. In other words, when you communicate, there should be a common understanding between the speaker and the listener about what is meant. When misunderstandings happen, it is because there is a breakdown somewhere in the communication system. The listeners heard something different than what the speakers thought they said.

Many of us speak without thinking. We have an idea and blurt it out. For example, you may be puzzling over a difficult question, and suddenly you see the person who has the answers walking down the corridor. You jump up to ask a question. If you don't get the answer you need, or the other person seems confused, it may have something to do with how you presented the information.

Communication starts in your own head. You need to be clear about why you are communicating. What do you want from the other person? Do you want the other person to do something, tell you something, or understand something? The point of communication is not what you say; it's what the other person hears.

Good communication starts with your own mental clarity. What, exactly, do you want? After you are clear on what you want from the other person or persons, the next step is to decide on your mode of communication. Sending an e-mail, compared to speaking with someone in person, for example, could produce vastly different results. If you want someone to do something, you also need to be clear about what, exactly, you want them to do, and how both of you will know when it is done.

An important thing to remember about communication is that people take more from your body language and tone of voice than they do from your words. If someone gets upset with you, and you do not know why, nine times out of ten it will be because of your tone or body language. This applies not only to in-person communication, but to telephone and e-mail communication as well. Abrupt telephone communication and curt e-mails lead to innumerable and unnecessary misunderstandings.

Probably the most important step in communication is the final one: ensuring that you have understood the other person, and that you have been understood by them.

You may be surprised how often communication, when not verified, can be like that childhood party game, "broken telephone", in which the first child in the line whispers a phrase to the second, who passes it to the third, and so on, down the line. Uproarious giggles erupt when the last child repeats the phrase, which sounds astoundingly unlike the original.

Listen

Surprisingly, your most important tool in working with others, whether communicating information, attempting to influence others, or even negotiating a contract, is not your mouth—it is your ears.

Have you ever seen two-year olds play together? They may play in the same room, but they do not play with each other. The play is parallel, each child in his or her own world, with his or her own toys. The only interaction happens if one child interferes with the other's toys or space.

Sadly, much adult communication happens in the same way. People enter a conversation with their own thoughts and intentions, and often stay on that track, regardless of what the other person says. While the other person speaks, they just wait for the person to take a breath, so they can continue what they were saying before.

People often attribute their inability to listen, or the lack of desire, to having no time. They feel pressured to complete something, and have no time to listen. They just want to say what they want to say, and run off. What we say, indeed what we think, can change dramatically depending on what the other person says. Listening for five minutes can often avoid a great deal of wasted time and energy later.

Suppose you are trying to convince a colleague to tackle a project your way. You have done projects such as these many times before, and you consider yourself quite an expert. Who is this person to challenge your way of doing things? So you just want to tell them how it is to be done, and get started. Time is of the essence! Your colleague has questions but you have no time for debate.

There are many reasons why you should give your colleague a few minutes of your full, undivided attention. By listening carefully, you will be able to analyze any problems, and possibly solve them on the spot, rather than run into them later. Perhaps the colleague does not understand something and needs clarification. Clarifying the details now could avoid him doing the tasks incorrectly. Perhaps the colleague has a novel idea that could save time. If that turned out to be the case, you would deeply regret not having listened.

Listening is a key tool in influencing and negotiating. People enter a negotiation scenario ready to sell their position. Their minds are so full of their own thoughts that they cannot hear you. The wise negotiator listens first. If you listen before you speak, you will learn the other person's perspective, and be able to take it into consideration. You can then incorporate their thoughts when you present your case. If the person feels heard, and he hears familiar ideas incorporated into your proposal, agreement comes much easier.

A last and most important element in listening is multi-tasking. Surely you have experienced trying to talk with someone while they are doing something else; for example, typing or reading. How did it feel?

Sharon does the following activity in her communication seminars. She asks people to speak, for one minute, to a partner who is pretending to not listen. The activity never lasts longer than 45 seconds because they can't do it. They cannot concentrate, they get frustrated and angry and find themselves performing all kinds of antics to get the other person's attention.

Even though it is just a game, they cannot stand it for even one minute. When Sharon repeats the exercise, this time with the partner paying attention, they complete the exercise, and finish communicating what they want to say before the minute is up. Sharon has done this activity with hundreds of people. Giving someone your full attention, especially if they are upset or confused about something, takes only a couple of minutes. You will be able to solve a problem, gain a new perspective, save time, and even succeed in a difficult negotiation; and all you did differently was to be patient, give the other person your full attention, and listen before you spoke.

Trust Yourself and Others

You are in a much better position to collaborate with others if you have done your personal homework. If you have taken the time to be clear about your skills, abilities, personal mission, and your contributions to your organization, you are standing on solid ground.

There will be occasions when your self-confidence is challenged. At these times, remind yourself of all the work you have done to define your strengths, and trust yourself. When we trust

"Leave gossip and blame to the insecure."

ourselves, it is much easier to trust others, because we do not see them as adversaries.

You may have heard the following proverb, which is attributed to Hillel: "If I am not for myself, who will be for me? If I am only for myself, then what am I? And if not now, when?" These three sentences are particularly apropos when developing the ability to trust yourself and others.

The first line encourages you to trust yourself, to be your own best advocate. If you do not believe in yourself, how can you expect others to believe in you? Our behaviour directs people how to treat us, as clearly as if we were wearing a sign on our forehead. If we treat ourselves with respect, and display trust in our own abilities, others will trust and respect us too.

Hillel's second line encourages us to stretch beyond ourselves. "If I am only for myself, then what am I?" In other words, what kind of a person are you if your only concern is for yourself? Hillel's second line encourages us to not only do for others, but also to trust and believe in others, to give them a chance. There are, of course, untrustworthy people, of whom we need to beware. We believe however, that most people have positive intentions. They just want to get their job done and go home at the end of the day with a sense of satisfaction. We believe they are working to the best of their ability. No one wakes up in the morning and consciously decides to make mistakes and create obstacles for others.

For trust to happen between two people, someone has to take the first step. Simply be open to others' positive intentions. Anticipate the best from them, and build on that trust by acknowledging their good work. Sincere trust takes time to build, but it has to start somewhere. Too many workplaces are replete with mistrust, criticism, gossip, and blame.

Hillel's last line reads, "If not now, when?" Be bold. Start today. Trust yourself, and be willing to develop trust in others; then watch the positive effect it will have on your career.

Be Considerate

Why do you need to be considerate of others? No matter where you work, you need other people. Even if you work alone in a small cubicle in a large organization, your work is connected with the work of others. The people with whom you have to interact, whether they are colleagues, administrative support, or managers, are there for a reason and deserve your consideration.

What does it mean to be considerate in the workplace? It means to show respect for, and value the people around you in the workplace. It means to recognize people for what they have to offer, especially if they bring skills to the table that vary significantly from yours. Everyone has as much right to their perspectives, and to their opinions, as you do, even if they baffle you sometimes.

Imagine that you were running your own business, and your colleagues, whose ideas and skills differ from yours, were now your clients whose business you required, how would you treat them? That idea is not such a stretch; in some form, we all serve each other, and if we could keep that in front of our mind, it would help us be considerate.

Another factor to consider is that people have different learning and communication styles. We forget that we see the world from one perspective only—ours. People often think that everyone sees the world the same way, and wonder what is wrong with the person who sees it differently. We tend to under-rate our own skills, because they come easily to us, and wonder why someone else does not have them.

Let us look, for example, at mathematics. If math comes easily to you, you will of course generalize that math is easy. Anyone who is not good at math would then, by your definition, be not particularly smart. Imagine that you are in a meeting and you are presenting a statistical analysis of something, and a colleague, even after asking many questions, remains baffled. How do you treat her? What words do you use? What does your tone of voice and body language convey?

Nobody likes to feel they are inadequate, and we all have areas in which we could be exposed as inadequate; have you ever called in a specialist to your home for a major problem, only for them to make a very minor adjustment, and it's fixed?

Be considerate of the differences in people, and don't be too quick to judge them based on what you think is obvious.

Small changes in behaviour are often all that is required to redirect your career toward success. Being considerate of others and treating them with respect will enhance the atmosphere of your work environment, and benefit your career immensely.

Process Disagreements

The key to managing disagreement positively resides in how you process the situation. Your conditioning dictates how you behave in a disagreement. The emotion that your conditioning generates is responsible for most of the friction present in a confrontation, more so than the difference of opinion about the subject. You want to be seen as someone who reacts well under pressure, who welcomes the opportunity to tease out the best solution to a problem. Having an internal process that you use to handle disagreements will help you to be more objective.

Every day, there are a variety of things in the workplace on which people could disagree. Since everyone has a unique perspective, disagreement provides the opportunity to explore different angles and come up with the best possible solution. The ability to deal effectively with disagreement will help you both personally and professionally.

Your internal reaction to disagreement will vary, depending not only on who is disagreeing with you, but also on how they express their disagreement. A person in authority disagreeing with you and a colleague disagreeing with you will produce different internal reactions, as will someone who speaks respectfully to you and someone who does not. From whomever and however the disagreement is expressed, recognize that your internal reaction is a reflex response. It is important to take a moment to allow your thinking processes to kick in before responding.

When involved in a disagreement, be open to accepting that the other person's opinion is valid from their perspective. A collaborative response involves being genuinely inquisitive, asking the person to elaborate, and then listening carefully. It is important when dealing with disagreement to be able to put your own thoughts aside for a moment, and look for the seed of truth in what the other person is saying. Look to generate a better solution, rather than defend your own; a solution that might incorporate both ideas.

Following a structured process when handling disagreements will create a win-win scenario, both personally and professionally. Your organization will have a better product and you will be seen as having a professional attitude. In addition, your colleagues will see you as someone who remains calm under stress, and who is a pleasure to work with.

WORKING WITH OTHERS SUMMARY

How you use your unique skills and abilities with others will tip the balance in your favour. You can be the most competent person in the workplace, but without the ability to work and play well with others, you will be forever hampered in your career.

Here is your quick reference table of all the abilities in this section, followed by the key positive behaviours that characterize them. The right column describes behaviours that are displayed when the ability has not been developed.

Abilities	Positive Behaviours	Negative Behaviours
Masters own communication	Easy to understand	Confusing
Listens	Great to talk with	Others never get their chance to talk
Trusts self and others	Trustworthy	Gossips, blames others
Is considerate	Easy to like	Disagreeable
Processes disagreements	Manages disagreement well	Defensive

Development

In the Development Stage, your career comes into a period of growth. You expand your abilities to contribute to the business. You also become more involved in the general growth of the business.

This stage contains the next two steps of the Career Acceleration Process.

Step 3: Progressive—Working effectively in a team environment

Step 4: Constructive—Increasing your influence on your business

Progressive

INTRODUCTION

The progressive level is very exciting. When you look back on your career, you will find that it was at this level of responsibility that things really started to happen for you. It is a very dynamic period because you start to see a vivid picture of where you are headed. Your career is in your hands now, and developing your abilities at this level will show an almost immediate return for your efforts.

Most people do not break into this level of responsibility. Maybe it is because they have had all forms of ambition driven out of them by others or by their circumstances. Most often, it is because they never properly developed the abilities in the levels of Functional and Collaborative required to move into this level. The good news is this: when you move up to this level you break free from the majority of the population. People at this level are much sought after. When you move into the Progressive level, you are entering a stage in your career that can be considered your launch pad. The Functional and Collaborative levels are critical, and must be mastered for a successful career, but it is not until you reach the Progressive level that your career starts to take shape.

At the Progressive level, you appear to others to be independent. You are willing to learn, and you clearly have a desire for more responsibility. If there is an important objective for the company to reach, you are very likely to be considered for the job. Your interests have noticeably widened. You find yourself more inquisitive about your own profession, beyond just how you can perform better. You also have an interest in finding out how others have been successful. You become aware that there are many universally known habits and behaviours that successful people employ. You discover new ways to analyze your own abilities and your HMw. It becomes clear to you that every level of responsibility includes refining all of your abilities from all previous levels.

If this all sounds like hard work to you, don't panic. You dictate the terms under which you develop your abilities. The more effort you apply, the greater the rewards, and the more quickly they will arrive. If you find yourself spinning your wheels at any time, refer back to the Functional level abilities in the Powering Up section to refresh your understanding of setting goals.

Providing your services to many is far easier if you have higher levels of responsibility. You generally become included in projects that carry a greater importance to the business. You find yourself involved in meetings with people of influence outside of your immediate working environment. These opportunities and others come not because of the competence you apply to completing your daily tasks, but because of the additional contributions that your abilities provide to your business. This is a critical lesson to understand; the opportunity to move your career forward is within your control. All you have to do is learn and implement the lessons provided in this chapter.

Contribute Beyond Your Boundaries—Step Forward

Once we realize that doing what other people expect us to do is only going to get us as far as other people want us to go, we come to a conclusion. Doing more than what is expected of us is a powerful way to increase our level of responsibility. Those who stand back while others extend themselves and contribute more don't understand that they are missing out on golden opportunities. People who want to rise in levels of responsibility are always on the lookout for how they can do more than their current obligations require. This means putting in that bit of extra effort, and volunteering for additional duties.

Stepping forward may be as simple as offering a colleague a helping hand or as complex as volunteering to research or take on a new and different project. It is important to get the reputation that you are a hard worker who is willing to go the extra mile to get the job done well. This alone will enhance your reputation immensely.

It is important to pay attention to how you step forward. You want to be seen by everyone as someone who is good to work with, who can be counted on, not only to complete tasks, but also to go beyond what is required. Step forward because you care about a project's success and because you want to do your best to make a difference. Your bosses and colleagues will be able to tell. Maybe you have worked with people who pulled their weight with gusto for the good of the company. You loved working with them. You may have also worked with people who were simply trying to impress, sometimes at others' expense. These people weren't fun to work with.

"What you do today that you are not paid for is an investment in your future."

Stepping forward is a way to show that you are the kind of person who will go the extra mile. You do it out of a genuine intention to help the business move forward. The extent to which you can add value to your presence in a job will have a direct impact on the additional responsibilities you will be asked to take on. People who contribute beyond their boundaries quickly become a valuable asset to their organization and opportunities are presented to them.

Be Open-Minded

People who are able to accept that there are many different ways to accomplish a task, are viewed as people who work with an open mind. By contrast, people who see only their way to accomplish a task are usually inflexible. When in positions of responsibility, this behaviour is often seen as "my way or the highway". These people limit their opportunity to provide excellence. They block out the significant resource of collective minds, and that certainly has an impact on what the company offers to the marketplace.

Keep in mind that the objective of an organization is to serve, whether it is a customer, a community, or a cause. Whatever the business purpose is, we work to serve, and in return, we achieve our personal objectives. Maintaining an open mind, and making use of all the ideas available to deliver the very best service, should be a standard mode of operation.

Being flexible and open to listening to other people's opinions on a subject has numerous benefits. Regardless of who offers their input or what their experience is, the benefits of being willing to hear the suggestions of others include showing respect for people (this alone is worth the price of admission), being exposed to different view points on a subject, accessing different experiences to apply to the subject, encouraging future thoughts from people who appreciate being included, and not being tied to your own perspective.

Here is an example that could have turned out very differently, had the approach not been open-minded. Colin had an issue relating to one of his company's suppliers who, for a long time, had provided an important service. The manager responsible for the supplier services presented compelling evidence to Colin that the supplier was contravening a company agreement. The manager recommended that the supplier agreement be cancelled. Colin contemplated the actions he would take and suspected that he would have to cancel all agreements with the supplier. As Colin's company was a major customer for the supplier, the consequences would be serious. Before speaking to the supplier, Colin chose to call a senior executive to get his opinion on how he would deal with this situation. Colin fully expected to hear confirmation of his own conclusion. But he was pleasantly surprised. The senior executive said to him, "In 99% of the cases, people are acting with genuine intent, and in this case, they may have made a mistake. If this turns out to be the case you can educate the supplier, and continue the relationship."

Colin met with the supplier. Without accusing the supplier, he outlined the evidence to support the concerns the company had, and then asked for comment. The supplier was stunned to hear of the concerns, and eagerly provided the other side of the story. It became very clear to Colin that the supplier had every intention of following the letter of the agreement, but they had been placed in a situation of conflict through no fault of their own. The supplier was visibly upset by the situation, and based on the concerns Colin raised, expected the relationship with Colin's company to be terminated. However, because of the advice Colin had sought before approaching the supplier, he entered the meeting with an open mind. Colin and the supplier created an acceptable plan that would resolve the issue, and the relationship was allowed to continue. In fact, going forward the relationship became far stronger and more beneficial to both parties. Colin called the senior executive back, and thanked him for his input.

Keep an open mind, and seek and value the input of others. Often, another insight can change the complexion of a situation, and create a much more favourable outcome.

Welcome New Experiences

Life would be so much easier if everything came out the way we wanted it to, and all of our experiences were happy and pleasant. But, in the real world, the sky isn't always blue, and the boss can be a real pain.

The wonderful truth about the experiences we have in life is that if we choose to, we can benefit from all experiences, whether they are comfortable or painful. This next anecdote illustrates the possibilities that you can extract from a poor situation.

Geoff was a bank clerk in the City of London. The bank he worked for was a commercial bank, and the vast majority of its customers were corporate accounts. Geoff was very new to his career—having left school to join the bank he was now in his second year of employment. One day, Geoff completed a large transfer for a corporate customer, moving money from one currency into another. Unfortunately, an incorrect foreign exchange rate was applied, and the bank ended up having to absorb a significant sum of money because of the error. Geoff was called into the manager's office, and he faced the first setback of his young career. He was demoted from his position as an accounts clerk, and was moved to a filing job. If Geoff had been more experienced, he would have realized that the manager was hoping he would just leave the bank, and try a different career.

Back when this episode occurred, much of the bank's customer information was kept in hard copy files. The task Geoff was asked to do was to change the cover of every paper file in the bank, of which there were thousands. It was estimated that the task would take about six months; clearly it would be very monotonous.

There is a very important twist to this episode. Rather than just taking the papers out of one file, putting them into a new file, printing the account name on the new file, and putting it back on the shelf, Geoff read the files; every one of them, and in detail. Within two to three months, Geoff had gathered more general knowledge about the bank customers than anybody else had in the branch. Soon, people were asking Geoff questions about the customers such as, "Who are this company's signatories?"; "What are the company signing levels?"; "What securities does the company hold with the bank?"

Geoff persevered and completed the job and accumulated a significant wealth of information about the bank's customers. When the filing job was complete, Geoff returned to his previous role.

Shortly after that, he was promoted to the position of Securities clerk. Geoff became the youngest junior manager in the bank.

The lesson from Geoff's anecdote is this: be on the lookout for possibilities in every situation. Even the direst of experiences often come with unique opportunities that can serve you well. Don't get stuck in lamenting your conditions; that is a sure way to remain stuck.

Expand Your Areas of Study

Regardless of what educational opportunities we had or didn't have growing up, we all have what might be an infinite capacity to learn. We learn better when we have an interest in a subject, and it is also easier to understand new material when the knowledge transfer is consistent with our own preferred learning style. Unfortunately, our early conditioning for learning, in many cases, is one of forced education. We had to do this, and we had to do it that way. If it wasn't fun or easy for you, it probably left a negative impression that you will later associate with anything considered to be education. The great news is that you can expand your areas of study based on what you want to learn, and you can learn it in a way that entertains you. You will discover that learning is not only enjoyable; it can take you to places that you didn't know existed.

Studying areas related to your job will give you a direct return on your time. But don't limit yourself; learning about sciences, history, mechanics, medicine, sports psychology, or anything that interests you will be of benefit, too. Frequently, knowledge we learn in one subject can be easily adapted to other subjects; in fact, it is amazing how often one field can introduce a direct benefit in another subject. This effect is what we want to focus on as we add variety to our contribution in the work force.

Being a lifetime student is not a chore, and as your career develops, you will recognize that continual learning is a very important ability that all leaders possess. If you want to move beyond your current level of responsibility, your decision to expand your area of study is not a matter of if, but when. Making the decision to do it now will be a key component in your acceleration process.

Attending seminars, listening to audio books, studying online, and reading from a multitude of sources about a variety of subjects will help you become a more creative thinker. The stories and subjects you will be able to talk about will add colour to your conversations, and make you a much more interesting person to be around. All leaders are readers, so if your career plan is to fulfill your potential, then join all the other leaders and expand your area of study.

 For further information on how to expand your areas of study, watch this free video. **http://bit.ly/1mhFJ5J**

Dare to Commit

There is an oft-repeated quote from mountain climber W. H. Murray that includes these words:

> *"...the moment one definitely commits oneself, then providence moves, too."*

> *"All sorts of things occur to help one that would never otherwise have occurred. A whole stream of events issues from the decision, raising in one's favour all manner of unforeseen incidents, meetings and material assistance, which no man could have dreamed would have come his way."*

We have found this quote to be the absolute truth. People who commit themselves to achieving something, succeed. But there are many people who do not commit. Two of the key reasons why people resist committing themselves to achieving what they want, are that they don't want to appear selfish, and they have not clarified their dreams.

Because we are told from early childhood to do what others want us to do, in the way that they want it done, we spend our lives trying to please others. As children, we are taught to please our parents. We marry, and try to please our spouses. We join organizations, and try to please our bosses. Then one day we wake up, and realize that we are miserable. We have lost sight of what we wanted to do, and we have been conditioned to think that following our own desires is selfish.

If we don't live "on purpose", it will cause stress in our lives, which often leads to physical illness. Sharon has heard this story countless times, while coaching people who had cancer. In her experience, people who got cancer had often put their own dreams on the back burner. It was as if they believed that wanting something for themselves was somehow bad. Part of their healing involved both giving themselves permission to have their own desires, and committing themselves to working toward them.

It is important for you to clarify your own dreams and commit yourself to making them come true. What do you want in your professional life? What are your highest hopes? Commit yourself and go for it. As W.H. Murray says, you will be amazed at what will happen.

We began this section with the first passages of a W.H. Murray quote. It seems fitting to conclude with the end of that quote:

> *"Whatever you can do or dream you can, begin it. Boldness has genius, power, and magic in it."*

Cultivate Reliable Sources

Creating a network of reliable sources, and accessing their experience and information, can give you a critical advantage in all aspects of your career. Seeking input for projects or ideas that you are working on will add value to your situation. You may get a point of view that exposes giant holes in your approach; problems that you hadn't thought of. You can then go back and plug the holes, or instead, move on to other brilliant ideas.

Reliable sources come in many different ways. The most obvious source is to consciously pick a few people that you know well. Perhaps they work in different departments; this would lend different perspectives to the feedback you get. Work hard to cultivate your relationship with these people. Even if you move on to different companies, stay in touch. As you all grow throughout your career, this group of diverse people can become a very valuable resource for you.

Some people might have the kind of information that you could use, but you find their personality off-putting. If you are able to look beneath the surface, they, too, can become reliable sources. Other reliable sources might be so well-disguised that you only find them by chance. These are often people who hide their light under a bushel basket.

There are many sources of reliable information. Always be on the lookout, and don't judge a book by the cover.

Marie was an internal consultant in an organization that was in the midst of a major downsizing. She was part of the human resources department, which consisted of over 900 people. Marie provided advice to senior management, and also headed a team of consultants who provided services across the country. She needed both access to current information, and mentors to guide her through the troubled waters ahead to be able to guide others effectively. Getting information to move this project forward would not be an easy task.

Unfortunately, her boss was insecure, and as a result, guarded information very carefully. For Marie, he was not an option for either information or mentorship, but two of his peers appeared to be. Marie developed a collegial relationship with both of these people. She met them regularly for either coffee or lunch and made a conscious effort to listen to what they were saying. They divulged a lot; clearly they trusted Marie, and she rewarded that trust by keeping their confidences.

However, her most reliable mentor and source of information came from an unexpected place. The president of the organization arranged a meeting with Marie to discuss the progress of the reorganization. In the course of this meeting, Marie met the president's executive assistant. They had never met before, but soon after their first meeting, the executive assistant gave Marie valuable information and advice that contributed significantly to the organizational transition.

The purpose of this anecdote is to demonstrate that we all need reliable mentors and sources of information. One person rarely holds all the answers to the adventures of business, and sometimes mentorship comes from a collage of people. To ensure greater success, take the time to seek and accept input from others. If you are able to form a reliable group of people who can help each other, work hard to sustain it. Make conscious choices about who you seek advice from, and be on the lookout for those who might be able to help, even from unexpected places.

Be Receptive

To produce at higher levels of responsibility, we must continually add value through stimulating suggestions and productive actions. This requires that we are on the alert for new and relevant information from outside of the usual confines in which we work. By "new", we don't necessarily mean unique or invented, we simply mean new to you. You will add your own unique perspective to the information you receive, and in doing so, you make it "new", too.

Being receptive to ideas and information from any source makes you open to useful insights from a multitude of daily occurrences. Taking this a step further, putting yourself in places and circumstances that will expose you to new sources of information can lead to a quantum leap forward for thoughts and inspiration.

To be receptive, you must have your current purpose in mind, and a determination to achieve it. There is a mind-blowing amount of information available from all sorts of media all day and every day. In order to recognize information of value, you must be able to filter out that which is not currently valuable to your current purpose.

Information, people, ideas—indeed, everything we need to further our current purpose is available to us all the time. We just have to be ready to receive it.

Melanie was a real estate sales person. She spent a number of hours over the course of her week driving from one property to another. Melanie decided to listen to ideas and suggestions about her industry on CDs during her driving time. She felt that her drive time was unproductive, and thought that perhaps she could use it to stimulate some thoughts. She listened to the stories of some of the top sales people in her industry, and gathered some very useful ideas that she could implement.

One day, when Melanie was looking for her next drive-time learning material, a friend gave her a set of discs that would help her to learn French. Melanie hadn't considered learning French before her friend gave her the CDs, but she thought, "I'll give it a go." The discs weren't the only source of French language training that she ended up taking, since one new experience often leads to further stimulating adventures. In just a few months, Melanie was quite capable of speaking French at a basic level. As Melanie lived in a bilingual area where French was quite common, her new ability created a very productive influence on her real estate business.

Because Melanie was receptive to new ideas and information, she was now able to present herself to an entirely new marketplace. As a direct result, she increased her business to the point that she was able to add an associate to her business to help deal with the increase.

Putting yourself in the path of new ideas, thoughts, and experiences, and being receptive to them, will add fuel to your career progress. It isn't necessary for you to always generate new ideas for yourself; there are plenty of great ideas out there waiting for you to discover and adapt to your own circumstances.

Manage Tasks

Is there a way to manage time so that we can have a few extra hours each morning before the hustle of the day gets into full swing? If there is, please tell us how!

Time management really comes down to task management and, to refine further, it is task priority management. If you can't make time for a meeting right now, it's because you are doing something that is more important on your priority list. Not knowing how to prioritize tasks may leave you unable to attend important events because you are busy doing something else. When we look at our lives, we may find this happens all too frequently.

How much of your time is spent completing tasks that ultimately have no bearing on your business? If you are brutally honest, you may find that most of your tasks are of the "make busy" variety. If they were not completed, no one would know, and it would make no difference.

Amanda was feeling a lot of stress. She was putting in long hours during the work day, taking work home at night, and working on the weekend. She had a young family, and her constant focus on work was costing her dearly; she would rather have spent evenings and weekends with her husband and their two young children.

Amanda decided to quit her job. She went to her manager and handed in her resignation.

Her manager was reluctant to accept Amanda's resignation; she was just too valuable to the business. Together they discussed what her issues were. Perhaps the manager should have known the stress Amanda was under, but he didn't, and it came as a surprise to him to hear how much time Amanda was devoting to her work.

It didn't seem right. Amanda's responsibilities were important, but she should not have to spend so many hours working just to keep up.

They formulated a plan to review Amanda's work, and Amanda agreed to withhold her resignation until the review had been completed.

Over the next week, Amanda made a list of all the jobs she had to undertake. As she worked through the week, she added the many miscellaneous tasks we all do, but don't count as part of our job— like keeping up with her e-mail, and taking various phone calls.

Amanda then divided the task list into three groupings: tasks that were critical to the role; tasks that weren't critical; and tasks that added no value to the role, but which she did anyway.

When her list was ready, Amanda sat down with her manager, and they reviewed it together. The manager added a further dimension to the tasks list tasks that were her responsibility, and tasks that weren't. It's amazing how readily we all are to take on tasks that really belong in other departments.

Together they compiled a list of tasks to delegate to other departments. Of those tasks that were left, they agreed on the tasks that were critical and must be continued. Then they divided the non--critical tasks into those that should be continued, and those that added no value, but were always done. They agreed to stop doing all of these tasks for at least a month, and then determine whether there was any obvious impact.

The net result of this exercise was that over half of the tasks Amanda had been doing were either deleted or delegated. Starting the following week, Amanda began new work hours, from 9:00 am to 3:30 pm. She stopped taking any work home. This experiment continued over the following month, and the result was a great success for both Amanda and for the company. Shortly thereafter, Amanda took a time management course, and learned a new system that helped her organize her work still further.

This is an interesting case study, because there were no negative consequences from stopping the work that was deleted from her list. It was now very clear that a significant amount of Amanda's time had been focused on tasks that had no value to the business.

If a task falls off your desk, and there is no crash when it hits the floor, it shouldn't been on your desk in the first place.

To expand your knowledge on how to manage tasks, watch this free video. **http://bit.ly/NuVmaE**

Develop Good Presentation Skills

Assuming greater levels of responsibility in your organization requires having effective presentation skills. You will have to be able to discuss issues of ever increasing complexity with various individuals who have different perspectives. You will also need to present these ideas in writing.

The thought of presenting to a group of people can be daunting, and can conjure up a plethora of fears. One of the main fears that people have is fumbling what they have to say and embarrassing themselves. The key to dispelling this fear is proper planning and preparation of both the content and style of presentation. If you are fully conversant with the subject matter and have a clear purpose for your presentation, it will increase your confidence. Ensure that your audience also understands the subject and objective of your presentation. When everyone is clear, it helps the presentation flow smoothly.

When designing your presentation, it is important to be able to take complex ideas and break them into manageable bites. Remember that you are the subject-matter expert, don't over-elaborate your material; don't expect your audience to be at the same level of knowledge that you are. Help your audience by having only one main idea per slide and a limited number of bullet points.

In developing your presentation, you will need to consider the best format. Oral presentations are perfect when it is important to inform and inspire a group of people. Oral presentations are also very good for the introduction of new products and new ideas, particularly when you need to sell an idea or product to a group. If you need feedback from the audience, oral presentations will allow you to capture the comments of those who think well aloud, and on the spot.

Complex ideas may be more efficiently presented in written reports. When these reports are circulated, individuals have the opportunity to read and digest the material, and offer comments. There may be instances in which presenting to others involves a combination of both oral and written approaches. Circulating a report or presentation summary before an event gives people the opportunity to consider the material in private, and prepare for the presentation.

As you move up the ladder of responsibility, the ability to present complex ideas both orally, and in writing, is critical. You will want to showcase your work, and share new and emerging work with others to gain their support, feedback, and input.

There are many methods for developing and improving both written and oral presentation skills. A combination of taking courses, reading books, and observing and learning from others will ensure your continued growth and improvement in this area.

Move Beyond Obstacles

You will run into obstacles; that is a given. The key is to stay focused on your objective.

Mark was the head of a large team in a government department that was writing protocols for potential new legislation. Since this was very important legislation, Mark's team included doctors, forensic psychologists, trauma counsellors, lawyers, policy writers, and other assorted government employees. Mark's biggest obstacle was that those in government kept changing their minds. One month he was told to go ahead full-steam, and the next month he was told that the legislation would never pass. How was he to keep his team, which numbered over fifty people, moving forward?

As we discussed earlier, good goal setting involves plans to achieve the goals, along with benchmarks against which to measure success. That is exactly what Mark did. He said, "Last month we focused on union consultations. At the end of the month, when we were done, we celebrated. Next month we consult with industry. We are enjoying what we do and we are doing a thorough job, so we feel successful regardless of whether the legislation is ever passed."

Mark found a way around his obstacles and kept going, and you must do the same. Whatever the obstacle, you need to be creative. "No" does not always mean "No"; it may mean, "Find another way."

Distractions are another common type of obstacle that can derail you from your objectives. Even if you love what you do, work can be boring sometimes, or just plain difficult, and distractions can be more fun. This is when you have to be disciplined. Sometimes you have to just buckle down and do what needs to be done.

Interruptions are distractions, too. If the interruption is important, deal with it, and get back on track as soon as you can. If the interruption is not important, then push it away and remain focused on your objective.

Obstacles, whether originating from management, colleagues, or your own desire for distraction, can be killers of great projects. Your goals are worth fighting for, so find ways to stay on track. Keeping your projects on track allows you to keep your career moving forward, too.

PROGRESSIVE SUMMARY

You have now pulled ahead of the crowd. The progressive level is where you take on additional responsibilities. Now you begin to stand out, and others notice. They seek you out and ask for your thoughts and opinions on various business subjects. You will probably also be included in important cross-departmental meetings.

Use the following reference table of abilities and key positive behaviors to ensure you realize your career dreams.

Abilities	Positive Behaviours	Negative Behaviours
Contributes beyond own boundaries	Volunteers for additional duties	Sticks to the contract
Open-minded; accepts multiple right answers	Sees and values others' point of view	My way or the highway
Welcomes new experiences	Always learning and growing	Stuck; unwilling to look beyond their current knowledge and experiences
Expands areas of study	Wide interests, abstract thinker, interesting	Always discusses same mundane things; adds nothing new
Dares to commit	Clear about goals and committed to action	Focused on everyone's goals but their own
Cultivates reliable sources	Knows how and where to get answers	Resists input
Is receptive	Always learning	Argumentative; resistant to new ideas
Manages tasks	Knows priorities, not hurried or overworked	Disorganized; misses deadlines, overwhelmed
Has good presentation skills	Can explain complex issues	Confused; avoids presenting
Moves beyond obstacles	Faces problems head-on; stays on track	Gets distracted; quits

Constructive

INTRODUCTION

At the Constructive level, your career is beginning to mature. You are still driven by your own desire to achieve, but you are now also starting to take an interest in the development of the business, and the growth of others. Often, this level in your career is influenced by your circumstances away from work. Your focus is no longer centred on yourself. You may be starting a family or getting involved in volunteer work in your community. Usually, the progress we make at work reflects our circumstances away from work, and the opposite is also true.

As you develop an interest in the way things work around you, your questions change. You are still looking for ways to improve yourself, but now you also start asking questions about your organization. It's as if you have surveyed your business landscape for the first time, and you begin to ask questions such as, "Why do we do things this way?"

Your desire to understand your organization and see it grow becomes as important to you as your own growth. When you talk about your business to customers, colleagues, suppliers, or others in general, you speak in terms of what your company offers to the public and why, as well as what you do there.

The Constructive level is generally where people define how much responsibility they want to achieve in their career. Not everyone wants to be a manager or an executive. The responsibilities that those levels bring are not appealing to everyone. Many prefer to remain focused on their own work rather than on that of others. There is no judgment to be made about your preferred level. Moving into management levels at which you do not feel comfortable is sure to add unnecessary stress to your life.

Equally, staying at your level when you are capable of moving to a higher level will also create stress for you, as you will always feel like you are under-achieving.

Not only does the Constructive level offer new opportunities for personal and business growth, it is also the level where you will reach a turning point in your career, clarifying for yourself where to aim from here.

Take Time for Thinking

Spending time thinking is a master-level habit, and once formed, is incredibly satisfying and productive. During the time we set aside for thinking, our greatest ideas and solutions present themselves. Thinking is the first "cause" in the "cause and effect" process of career acceleration.

We all have the ability to think. What eludes most people is the discipline to schedule uninterrupted time, and the focus on what to contemplate. Too often, we become so embroiled in our daily work, fighting fires and meeting deadlines, that we simply don't take the time for thinking. Yet, order and improved productivity of our activities can be established by contemplation. Thinking about the outcome we desire for a particular scenario, rather than reacting randomly to obstacles, often provides the answers that otherwise would have been beyond reach.

Of course some situations require immediate, urgent action and don't allow for the luxury of time to think. But you can be sure that, if you don't schedule the time to think, you will have to spend more time fighting an increasing number of fires.

Andrew is a senior executive at a well-known international corporation. In the early years of developing his part of the business, completing his everyday tasks was more than enough to keep him busy for his full work day. As he became more efficient at performing his tasks he found additional time in his day for "not-urgent" activities. Andrew started to schedule time for deliberate, purposeful thinking. He closed his office door and contemplated specific objectives. Later, as he became more accustomed to his perfect thinking environment, (including time of day, location, even his mood), he started considering things from a broader perspective.

One day, as he reflected, he realized that his daily tasks had gone down significantly to the point he was only spending about four hours a day to complete them. The majority of his day was now spent purposefully contemplating projects, both current and future, and ways to implement them. He even had a passing thought that perhaps he should take on more tasks (many people define being busy as working continuously on one task or another), but he quickly abandoned this unproductive line of thinking.

From the time Andrew started spending time thinking purposefully about go-forward productivity, he can clearly identify material consequences. The actions from his thinking time can be directly linked to the incremental production of millions of dollars in profit for the company's shareholders, and a significant increase in customer and employee satisfaction.

Taking the time to consider a project or process can often result in a change of direction or refinement that can save significant time in the implementation process. It might provide a higher quality result and even reduce overhead costs in reaching the outcome.

In addition, you will find that the time you spend thinking becomes precious and invigorating. The choices for the project or process to contemplate are unlimited. From a workplace objective, to your career aspirations, to resolving a relationship problem with a colleague or partner—all of these issues can be improved through deliberate, purposeful thinking.

Study Your Business and Industry: Become an Expert

To get ahead of the crowd and rise up the ladder of industry, we need to take our profession seriously, whatever that profession may be. If you have not yet made a point of researching your industry, take this advice; research your business and your industry. What you learn will pay you dividends way beyond the cost of this book.

Do not delegate decisions about your intellectual growth to your company, your HR department, or your manager. It is up to you to ensure you get the right training to allow you to move up to the next level of responsibility. Do you think that someone else will take care of you? Leaving these decisions to others is a big mistake. Your company, your manager, and your HR department may do their best to help you grow your abilities and expand your world view; we encourage you to look at this only as a nice benefit. Your development is your responsibility; it cannot be delegated.

We often hear people say, "My company doesn't invest enough in my training", or "Imagine, they want me to take training on my own time!" This kind of thinking will sentence you to a lifetime of underachievement.

David was a top producer in his company, and one of his rewards was to take a training course of his choice. The course he picked included speed reading, and this quite appealed to David. The course turned out to be a lot deeper and broader on points of self-development than David had anticipated.

This opened the floodgates for David, and he discovered that he really wanted to continue learning about himself, and his business and industry. Over the next few years, strongly influenced by that first course, David's career took off.

Studying your business and your industry should not be optional. David's course cost about $1,000. If that $1,000 had been invested in a regular savings account, in 10 years he might have doubled his money. David can confidently say that, as a direct result of that course, and the influence it had on his career, he has made significantly more than $1,000,000 from that $1000 dollar intellectual investment.

Value Progress Over Praise

Your success, however you define it, does not come from what you receive. Your success comes from what you give. Too often, we meet people who have confused their purpose at work. Many people think that they work only to receive an income, and they don't realize that this mindset is creating many roadblocks to fulfilling their potential.

With a different mindset—working to expand the business' reach, and the satisfaction of customers—your contribution becomes far more effective, and the rewards you receive usually reflect this change.

When we understand that the key to progress is not receiving, but giving, we are more likely to work without the need for personal praise. That is not to say we are trying to deflect praise—it's always nice to know our work is valued—but the need for praise will create issues.

When we work instead to provide a better service, we are more likely to be open to sharing our thoughts and current progress. There is no need to protect our contribution, or to be overly sensitive about the release of information. Being service-focused will attract the ideas and opinions of others, and the results will improve accordingly.

Praise from others follows nature's laws. If you pursue praise, it runs away from you. If you give praise, it comes back effortlessly. If you put your best efforts forward in a genuine attempt to improve your service, then other people's praise of your work is no longer necessary. There is only one person who needs to be satisfied with your efforts, and that is you. Of course, if others aren't pleased with your output, you'll likely hear it soon enough. If you are confident that you sincerely applied your best effort, you can be equally confident in gracefully accepting negative feedback, even if it is not well-delivered.

Remain focused on the company objectives, consistently work to provide your best service, and strive to create an environment of progress. This mindset will make you more effective, and although you are not searching for it, you are likely to receive more praise.

For more information on how to value progress over praise, watch this.
http://bit.ly/1gAQGXN

Push Your Envelope

Pushing the envelope is a term used when increasing the maximum capability of an aircraft. An aircraft is repeatedly flown higher and faster until the maximum capability has been reached. Engineers then go back to the drawing board and refine the aircraft, pushing the envelope further.

You too have capabilities that must be tested, and when you reach your maximum, you will learn what it takes to move to the next level. There is a major obstacle that most people do not overcome, however, and this is why most people don't push their own envelope: they don't have to!

It's a lot easier to stay where you are, and not push for improvement. But that means that you get trapped in your comfort zone and you continue to perform at significantly lower levels than you are capable of producing.

Comfort zones are largely the product of two innate conditions. The first is linked to the pain and pleasure principle. This principle drives us to move away from pain and toward pleasure. A key aspect of this principle is immediacy. The more imminent the pain or pleasure is, the more likely we are to act. Avoiding pain is the dominant condition, and we become good at moving away from it. In fact, we will go to enormous lengths to avoid pain, including giving up pleasures that could come from accepting some pain in the short term.

If you avoid the pain of confrontation with an aggressive colleague or manager (short-term pain), for example, you accept an unpleasant working environment as your ongoing reality.

All of the conveniences around us make it easy for us stay in our comfort zones. For example, if you can't be bothered to prepare a healthy meal, you might, instead, go to a drive through restaurant and pick up some fast food. Then you justify your poor choice by thinking, "This one time won't hurt." But it doesn't take long for the cumulative effect of convenience to cause your living conditions to drop below what is necessary for you.

The second innate condition is our adaptability and tolerance to accept new, and even undesirable, conditions. Imagine a road on your route to work is under construction and you have to take a lengthy detour each day. After the initial annoyance, you quickly become familiar with the new route and you become tolerant to the inconvenience. If the construction lasts for very long, you will eventually accept the new condition and hardly think about it.

The pain and pleasure principle, combined with our ability to adapt and tolerate negative conditions, cause us to accept situations far below that which we could aspire to. It is very likely that there are things you could do to improve your situation at work, but because the changes come with an element of pain, or the improvements are not immediately pleasurable, you avoid making any changes.

It is probable that the consequence of not pushing your envelope is that you are limiting your opportunities. This could end up costing you hundreds of thousands of dollars through your career. It also means that you fall short of achieving your full potential, and that is a great shame for you, and for all the people that would otherwise have benefited from your best service.

The secret to breaking free of the conditions that leave you rooted to your comfort zone is to anticipate the pleasure that you will experience if you increase your ability, and fulfil your potential.

What would the rewards allow you to experience? Perhaps you could pay for your children's college fees, switch to flying business class, or sit in a stadium or theatre box to watch a world class performance.

Perhaps you would choose to run your own business, or create a charitable foundation for a cause you care about. To experience the pleasure, think about a desire that burns inside you, and imagine what it would feel like to experience fulfilment of that desire.

If you take a flight somewhere, walk through the first class section. Volunteer at a charity organization for one day. Whatever it is, if you can create a clear image in your mind of the pleasure that fulfilling your potential will bring to you, it will motivate the desire within you to do what might otherwise seem uncomfortable, and easy to avoid.

Settling in to your comfort zone is largely a result of the pain and pleasure principle. It is compounded by your adaptability and tolerance of current conditions. These may well be the primary reasons why so many people do not come close to achieving their full potential.

Push the outer edge of your envelope. Create an image of your desire that can be with you at all times. It is this image that will help you break free of your comfort zone, and drive you to fulfill your potential. If you have any doubts about achieving your dreams, consider this: life is not random—you wouldn't even think it if you couldn't do it. Break free of your comfort zone and reach for the sky!

New Problems Require New Solutions

It's very easy to get stuck in a particular way of thinking. Problems appear or objectives are set, and the common reaction is to try and fit what is currently available to meet the new challenge. This kind of thinking can be like trying to force an existing square peg in to the newly formed round hole. This can cause weeks, months, or even years of frustration as the business chronically falls short of expectations. This can cause a major disruption to some or all of the work force in the company who are unable to achieve their goals.

We don't need to always reinvent the wheel, but sometimes we need to recognize that new solutions are required for our new problems.

A UK business that had territories covering mainland Europe was enjoying well-earned loyalty from its UK customers. However, revenue from the international territories had been largely flat for many years. The sales approach that worked for the UK just didn't seem to be making any impact in the international territories.

Because the international territories were only a small proportion of the business, this business line was largely ignored by the management team. However, when the economy turned sour and the competition intensified, the UK business became more difficult to maintain, let alone grow. The need to develop mainland Europe became a higher priority.

At first, the efforts were concentrated on increasing the focus on what they were already doing. Management began to review the international numbers, and speak more urgently to the sales people about them. Speaking louder about a subject does sometimes work; if the managers aren't commenting on a subject, then it isn't seen to be that important. But that kind of management doesn't usually create solutions for new problems.

Eventually, a serious planning effort was undertaken. The first change was made after reviewing the compensation plans for the sales representatives. Each rep had a major share of their territory in the UK with a small segment of international territory added on. In total, each rep had about a 90-10 split, with 90% being in the UK. If the rep did not achieve target in their international territory, it would usually be made up from their UK earnings. At worst, the losses were small enough that no one worried about them.

Clearly this was not a good situation for the company, and was the single biggest reason for flat revenue over recent years. Going forward, new sales positions were created that were 100% compensated by revenue growth from each international territory.

Other changes included a dedicated international sales manager, more regional meetings between sales reps and customers, more country-specific marketing, and more cost-efficient supply chains. Third-party reseller partnerships, which had previously not been seriously considered, were developed. Special customer programs were implemented, and specific reports were set up to track everything.

When the changes were complete, the international business had become a separate entity within the UK business. The result of these initiatives saw international revenue climb over 100% in the next couple of years.

None of these changes was rocket science. The critical change was that the UK business broke out of its usual mode of addressing the problems. The solutions implemented were realistic, practical, and most of all, new to this company.

Improvise, Test, and Create Paths for Others

Process is important in all areas of life; whether you are following the processes of your company to fulfil its mission, or you are following the Career Acceleration Process to develop your own abilities. Understanding the value of process is critical to the successful achievement of an objective.

However, no process should be so rigid that it cannot be amended to reflect changing conditions. If you have a procedure that follows A, B, C to get you to D, you will be able to analyze the process, if at some point, you don't get to D. Perhaps conditions have changed and B needs to be amended—and after that has been done, the process will work well again.

As we have discussed, new problems require new solutions. This can seem scary to some people, while others won't even consider doing something new unless someone else authorizes it. If you are contemplating changing a process of consequence at work, it should be tested under controlled conditions before being rolled out for production (whatever you are producing).

It is the testing aspect of trying new things that we want to cover in this section. Trying new things doesn't have to be a hopeful shot in the dark. In fact, that approach rarely produces any benefit. Being creative involves the conscious contemplation of completing established objectives in new ways or contemplating completely new objectives. Being able to generate innovative processes that lead to repeatable success requires producing clear processes. For workers to follow the new processes, they will need to know what to do, how to do it, and what outcomes they should expect. If we boldly try new things and then we are unable to repeat them, it becomes very difficult to replicate the effect, and impossible to teach to others.

If we create a habit of testing new processes in controlled conditions, we can generally minimize the risk. The idea is formulated, the outcomes are calculated, and a test is created. If the outcome is positive, the test can be repeated under broader conditions, and if outcomes can be verified, the new process is ready to be rolled out to the entire community.

This approach might sound rather sterile compared to the "shoot from the hip" style of progression, and there are occasions when it might be fun to be impulsive and see what happens. But if there are material consequences involved, it may be that the gun will get stuck in the holster, and you will shoot yourself in the foot!

In all seriousness, though, following a test methodology will actually encourage the inclination to try new things, knowing that the outcome is under control.

We should all feel bold enough to experiment; it is a great way to add spice into our lives. You never know what you or your company is capable of unless you push the outer edge of the envelope occasionally. Testing new methods not only controls the outcome, it also lays down the procedures for others to follow where your success leads.

Applying the ability to improvise, test, and create new paths for others demonstrates an important step forward in your level of responsibility. Recognizing the need to verify a successful new approach and defining how others can follow the approach is very beneficial to your business.

Pay Attention to Serendipity

In the complex and tightly interrelated universe we live in, can there really be anything as random as a coincidence? Perhaps we classify random but connected events as coincidences because we are unable to see the bigger picture from our level of perception. Or perhaps we just assign the word so that we don't have to think about what the cause really is. What we can say for certain, though, is that we have all experienced coincidences, and sometimes they can seem quite mysterious.

But what if there are things we can do to create beneficial coincidences? If you can agree that thoughts are causes, then perhaps you can accept that your thoughts can create coincidences that benefit your career. Indeed, coincidences aren't unexplained random happenings; they are caused very deliberately to bring what you need into your world, when you need it.

As empowering as that concept might sound, unfortunately it is still a stretch for most people to accept. If it is a stretch for you, then try this: the next time you experience a coincidence, consider the conditions that led to it. Perhaps you were thinking of speaking to a friend and the phone rang, and it was your friend calling you. Whatever the situation, consider what might have caused the coincidence.

The next step in using coincidences for your career benefit is to look for coincidences to happen. For example; if you need to see a particular customer, think of all the possible ways that the customer might present himself to you. Don't be shocked to find that, after doing this, you find yourself standing in a grocery checkout line behind your customer!

Being aware of everyday unplanned circumstances, and thinking about how they might benefit your cause, is extremely valuable in developing your career. Expecting coincidences that will further your career is an ability that, if you can accept it, can generate very beneficial circumstances for you. Those who rise to higher levels of responsibility are able to see value in coincidences, and use them to their advantage. In fact, many leaders agree that coincidences don't exist at all. The cause may be disguised somehow, but the effect is clear.

Coincidences happen all the time. Be aware that unexpected opportunities to further your goals can present themselves at any time, and take many different forms. A wise person is able to recognize, and find ways to benefit from, these situations.

Capture Your Thoughts

Many good ideas never come to fruition because they are lost in the mists that shroud our memory. How many times have you had an idea that you thought was so remarkable you'd never forget it, and then you did? Thinking on paper is a very good habit to cultivate. Whether you are formulating a new idea or contemplating actions, writing your thoughts on paper will ensure that you not only remember, but also organize them. Since we typically don't think in a logical order, random parts of a concept reveal themselves when they are ready. If we rely on our mind to organize the order of our thoughts, we will likely reduce the importance of certain thoughts, and probably lose them.

After writing your thoughts on paper, your mind is now emptied of the creative concepts, and the analytical side of your mind will be ready to go to work. You can view your idea with more objectivity, and be able to put your thoughts into logical order without worrying about blocking other creative thoughts. Reviewing your thoughts in this way will allow you to see the gaps in your initial thinking, and will stimulate your creativity, helping to expand your ideas.

Question your own thoughts. This may sound strange, but it is amazing how a few well-defined questions will lead to more productive thoughts. The results from this step may give you a much clearer picture of how to proceed. It will also enable you to better communicate your concepts, allowing you to give better direction to those who may be involved with the implementation of your ideas.

It is also useful to keep what you have written. Later, when reviewing a project or action stimulated by your thoughts, you can check whether the outcome met the original objectives, or where the implementation went off in a different direction.

Keep in mind that some ideas arrive before their time. Perhaps you saw subtle signs of a future situation, or you had foresight that stimulated your creative thoughts. If your thoughts can't be implemented today, perhaps they will fit a future situation.

Thinking on paper ensures that you capture your ideas, order them, and expand on them. Filing them for the future allows you to keep track of your ideas for use when the time is right.

Take Notes

As easy as it is to forget your own thoughts, it is even easier to forget someone else's. When beginning an important conversation, be sure to have a way of taking notes. There are many different ways that this can be of benefit.

If you are in a conversation with a senior member of staff, taking notes shows a great deal of respect; it shows that you want to be sure not to miss any of the wisdom being shared. If you don't take notes, the person you are talking to may be concerned that you do not fully understand.

The person you are listening to may make a comment that stimulates your thinking. It is rude to interrupt the person speaking, but it is easy to forget your thought. Writing a note ensures that you do not forget the thought, and will enable you to share it, or ask a relevant question, at the appropriate time.

When talking to a worker who reports to you, you may hear a comment that makes you think of an item that requires action by the staff member. Taking a note of the required action will not only help you to remember what it is, it will also show the other person that

> *"Be the one who leaves with all the good stuff."*

you can follow up on your requests. A manager who keeps notes of conversations and agreements about tasks to be completed will quickly get a reputation as someone who can't be fooled. If a worker challenges the agreement to complete a task and the manager pulls out the notebook and says, "Here it is: Tuesday last, we agreed that you would...." Normally, the employee then recalls the obligation and apologizes for the misunderstanding. That scenario will probably only occur once.

An action item raised in conversation might also be an action that you need to complete yourself. Taking a note will help you remember what is needed, and the parameters agreed to. If your manager insists that you agreed to complete a certain task by a certain date and you are sure it is not due for another week, you can politely challenge. "I am sure we agreed to the completion next week, but I may be wrong. Let me check my notes."

When you respond that way, your manager may be thinking, "Uh oh - I've been found out!" Your manager is also less likely to try that trick on you again.

During conversation, you will often encounter unexpected and useful comments. Being alert to the possibility of useful information, and being prepared to take notes, will ensure that you keep the good stuff for later, when you are ready to use it.

Prepare for Choice

A uniquely human feature is the ability to contemplate and select from a wide variety of choices. The evolution of the human race is defined by challenges and the subsequent responses. This also applies to your career; you face a challenge and you respond. In this section, we will discuss the important step between the challenge and the response—the choices available to your response. Some situations offer a limited number of choices, but most come with an abundance of choices, limited only by knowledge of the environment and creativity.

Our choices are often automatic, largely influenced by the experiences stored in our HMw, and by the environment we work in. The most frustrating response to a challenge is, "We will do it this way because that's how we have always done it."

Even if we are stuck in HMw auto-obedience, or we are limited by the local customs, occasionally we are faced with a challenge that requires a new conscious decision. Perhaps on the way to work, a road closure forces you to pick a new route. You will still draw on your knowledge of the area, but because there are choices available, and your choices are not dictated by what other people want you to do, the decision about which route to take becomes uniquely yours to make.

Choices that relate to less important responses, like the route to take to work, are not particularly stressful. But when it comes to the important things, like your career choices, for example, most people defer to others, or try to avoid making a choice at all. Refusing to make a decision will severely limit your career.

Make sure that you are prepared to make your choices. Being prepared requires that you have a clear understanding of your values and principles. You need to be conscious of your goals, and as educated as possible about the outcomes of your choice.

When you look back on your career, you will see that the choices you make between the challenge and your response is what directed your career. To the extent that you can, be prepared to consider your choices.

Use Your Products Creatively

A product or service is generally designed for one or more specific purposes. Organizational processes are designed to deliver the service to meet the specific needs the service is designed for. There may be opportunities, however, to serve customers in different ways using the same service. When contemplating ways to increase revenue, improve profit margins, or use otherwise useless inventory, be sure to think beyond your core business for your product or service.

Jenna was selling advertizing space in a well-known weekly journal. Even in good times, some space remained unsold; this space is called "open position" and requires the insertion of filler content. To Jenna, it always seemed like a waste that the filler space was not used to their benefit. After the deadline had past, the unsold space was gone forever. It could never be sold again.

Jenna contemplated how she could use the space to some positive effect. She designed a program to target large companies that might be attracted to her journal, but that were not currently customers. Calculating the average filler space available, she offered it on a "space available" basis. The opportunity she offered was to buy the space at a 70% discount. This was an offer that new customers couldn't resist.

The only drawback for the customer was that the publisher couldn't guarantee when the advertisement would run. The process was managed so that the offer would only be made with some degree of certainty that the ad would run in the next two or three issues. In addition to the 70% discount offer, a regular discount was also offered to the new customers. If they wanted to guarantee a spot in the current journal, they could do so at a modest discount.

The outcome from this program went beyond a significant reduction of filler space. Of the twenty or so targeted companies for the offer, all of them became loyal customers. Only a couple of them remained "space available" customers; the rest were converted to regular advertisers. Two of the targeted companies went on to become among the highest revenue producers for the journal for the long term.

This is a great case study to show how the creative use of your product can generate benefits beyond your expectations.

Remodel New Ideas to Fit

Sometimes, the ideas that come to us completely satisfy the situation. Unfortunately, that isn't always the case. In the same way that the first draft of a report is rarely the same as the final report, ideas can require modification before they fit the situation well. Be sure to be creative when receiving ideas. Do not ignore ideas based on the source, and don't condemn an idea too quickly, if at first it does not seem to fit the requirements.

A company in the IT services sector was looking for ways to generate customer advocates. Separately, the company needed to improve cash flow. A program was designed that would meet both requirements. By offering unlimited services for an annual upfront fee, the program guaranteed that purchasers would experience the company services multiple times, over an extended period. According to customer feedback, the services provided were excellent, so the company was confident that it would generate customer advocates who would share their experiences within their organizations. Receiving advance payment for the services would also significantly improve cash flow.

In the first year the program was well-received, but it created significant headaches, too. Offering unlimited services proved to be problematic. First: some of the advocates became very demanding, and while this was to be expected, at least to some degree, in many cases the demands went beyond reason. Second; the company had no experience to enable them to project the use of the services. As the offer was for unlimited use, they did project a high take-up of the services, but once they were up and running, they found that the average use was much greater than expected.

They were happy that the program was well-utilized, but the headaches and lower than expected profits meant that the program had to be amended, if it was to be continued.

Having designed a program that clearly had market appeal, going forward, the company now had the easier task of improving on the original idea. Over the following five years, the program was refined a number of times, and hybrids of the initial idea were created.

From a great idea that had some real teething pains, the program was eventually refined into something that made a significant contribution to the company's growth and long-term sustainability.

CONSTRUCTIVE SUMMARY

At the Constructive level, you are still driven by your own desire to achieve, but now you are also interested in the development of the business and the growth of others. Indeed, your desire to understand and see your organization grow becomes as important as your own growth.

For further guidance, use the table below. It lists the abilities discussed in this chapter and the key positive behaviours associated with each ability. The negative behaviours listed in the last column are those exhibited when the abilities are not present.

Abilities	Positive Behaviours	Negative Behaviours
Takes time for thinking	Considerate; prepared	Reacts on impulse; defensive; egocentric
Studies the business	Develops business expertise	Uninformed, gives unverified advice
Values progress over praise	Service-focused	Ego comes first
Pushes the envelope	Always trying to improve	Stuck in their ways
Seeks new solutions to new problems	Has progressive ideas and assigns new responsibilities	Averse to change
Improvises, tests and creates paths for others	Discovers opportunities and provides clear direction	Creates plans that are difficult to follow
Pays attention to serendipity	Takes advantage of the unexpected	Sees things as unlucky or unfair
Captures own thoughts	Retains and builds on ideas	Starts projects but doesn't finish them
Takes notes	Takes notes and refers to them	Rarely remembers what is said
Prepared for choice	Cool under fire	Has limited options; panics
Uses products creatively	Always open to seeing new angles	Limits use of product
Modifies ideas to fit	Continually reviews options	No idea is good enough

Delivery

In the Delivery Stage, you move into a period of your career where you are responsible for many people and the well-being of your organization.

In this stage, you learn how to lead people and business. You will also learn how to provide strategic direction for your organization.

This stage contains the next two steps of the Career Acceleration Process.

Step 5: Leadership—Leading people and business

Step 6: Executive—Learning about strategic direction

Leadership

INTRODUCTION

Being a leader requires a set of abilities that are developed—often over many years—and includes insights gained from many, sometimes significant, experiences. Some people deliberately develop their leadership abilities, while others find themselves thrust into a position that requires leadership abilities. Whatever the reason you find yourself in a leadership position, there is nothing more stimulating for others than working with a leader who has clearly defined abilities. It is true that some people have natural leadership tendencies. We see early evidence of this in the school yard. However, to be successful at a high level of responsibility requires more than the innate abilities that you may have been blessed with. And just being in a position that requires leadership abilities doesn't mean that a person has the abilities necessary to fulfil the role. A capabilities gap at this level is usually painful for everyone involved.

The Leadership step is divided into two sections. The first section is Leading People. In this section you will learn how to motivate people and manage what they do.

The second section is Leading Business. In this section you will learn how to take care of your business.

LEADING PEOPLE

Leading people carries with it a great deal of responsibility. People depend on you for guidance. Your position carries a degree of authority which can affect people's lives in good or bad ways, depending on your need to build your ego, your general abilities, and your intent. How you present yourself and act under the situations and conditions you encounter will be seen as an example for others to follow, or to challenge.

Before moving into your leadership position, your contributions were evaluated primarily on your ability to perform your tasks. Now, possibly for the first time, people will question your principles and values as well.

Your communications skills must now be developed to a higher standard. Your position is likely to require discussions about good and bad situations. Hiring, firing, performance evaluations, growth targets, and implementation of strategic plans all require specific abilities. How you communicate the objectives to your people can have a greater influence on the outcome than how the tasks are performed.

As a leader, you need to vary your working style, depending on who you are working with. Generally, you define how and when your people will connect with you. Understanding why specific people act as they do plays a big role in how you work with them. To gain this understanding, you must suspend your opinions, review prior evaluation notes, and actively listen to others around you.

Leading people can be the most satisfying role that you will ever take on. It can also be the most frustrating. Keep in mind that the frustration is certain to go both ways, and most of your problems will talk back.

Take the time to really get to know your people—cutting corners in this area will not save you time. Ultimately, the better you know your people, the more likely you will be a successful leader.

Hire Well

The job applicant arrives for the interview with you. He is nicely dressed and groomed, prepared to take notes, and he is carrying a binder full of company information to prove that he has done his preparation. This is the third and, hopefully, final interview in the process. The applicant is shown in to a now familiar meeting room, and with a glass of water in front of him, he nervously awaits the hiring manager. The hiring manager walks in and with a reassuring smile she places her file folder on the desk and opens it to reveal several sets of notes.

In the file there is an application form, a profiling test and an aptitude test, all completed. There is a list of references to be called, which will occur once the process has been finalized and only if the applicant has been selected. There is a job specification, not just the tasks to be undertaken but also the company objectives that the position will be responsible for. Next there is a skills and behavioural check list; these are the services that the company is looking to find in a successful applicant. Then there are the notes from the prior two interviewers.

There is a good deal of consistency between the sets of notes because all the hiring interviewers met at the beginning of the interview process to be sure they were all clear on exactly what they needed to know to make an informed decision. Included in their questions to the applicant were those that clarified the applicant's reason for wanting to work with their company, what he was looking to accomplish, and what needs he had to fulfil.

After the hiring manager settles in, she begins her questions. Of course, she has read the file prior to the meeting and is familiar with the process to date. The interview lasts for about an hour and includes a 15-minute presentation by the applicant giving his understanding of the first 30, 60 and 90-day expectations in his new job, as well as a brief overview of opportunities in the market place that he has researched.

After the interview, the interviewer thanks the applicant for his time and for his active participation in the process, and tells him that he will be advised of the decision before the end of the week. After the hiring manager has collected her thoughts and reviewed her notes, all of the interviewers meet for a final discussion about the applicant, and decide whether to offer him the position, or continue on with the process.

Unfortunately, the hiring description described above is not usually followed. More typical is a random approach. There is often a well-defined process for locating applicants and following up with applications, testing, and references. What is typically missing is an agreement among the interviewing managers about the approach and type of questions to be used in the interview meetings.

Too often, a hiring manager will complete a task a few minutes before the interview, grab the applicant file, march quickly to the meeting room, and then look at the file for the first time after greeting the applicant. The questions he asks are usually thought up on the spot, based on the applicant's file. These questions may be stock questions that are asked for every position, and in every interview. Sometimes, there are no questions or answers of consequence, and the interview is over very quickly. This may be a slight exaggeration, but unfortunately, it's not too far from the truth, in many cases.

Your people are your company's most important assets. Hiring decisions are arguably the most important decisions you will make, and having a collaborative strategy with everyone involved in the hiring process will pay significant dividends. No matter what urgent tasks you have to perform just before the interview, make sure to take the time to properly perform the process. If this means that you have to cancel an interview at the last minute, do so. After you explain that the urgent task had to be completed, and that the interview is too important for anything less than 100% of your attention, the applicant may be more impressed than he would have been if you had been unprepared, and rushed through the interview.

Be sure that your company follows a consistent and thorough hiring process. Interviewers should coordinate the objectives so that the questions and responses from each meeting will have a degree of objectivity and relativity. Whatever the starting salary for the position is, the cost of the time you invest to hire properly is easily justified by the cost of selecting the wrong candidate.

Create Team Spirit

People like to band together around a common objective; this creates a binding team spirit. People are more willing to go beyond the standard expectations when they clearly understand what the objective is, why it exists, and how they will, collectively, achieve it.

Working in silos of silence, and individually plugging away at whatever job description has been supplied without really understanding how the service fits into the bigger picture, is a sure way to limit the contribution of your company's most valuable asset—the staff.

We could give you many examples in which severe adverse conditions created a community spirit unequalled by anything previously experienced, and which led to extraordinary accomplishments. Why does this happen? Because there was a common objective, everybody pulled together and worked for the good of the broader cause. Everyone knew what was needed, and with clear leadership for how it would be achieved, there were no obstacles too large to overcome. In these extreme cases, one thing stands out; the people were in it together, and they pulled together. The credit for any achievements belongs to the group.

Fortunately, we are not always faced with extreme conditions. But it is possible and desirable, even without extreme challenges, to create community spirit that brings everyone together, and pulling in the same direction. People willingly follow orders if they recognize that what they are being asked to do is consistent with the objective of the business, which is to provide value to their customers. Everyone in the company has a role to play and everyone receives a reward commensurate with their role in achieving that end. Your message to your staff should be similar, regardless of how senior your responsibility is, or what role you play in the company. Leading a business, a department, or a section within a department should follow the same rules; every component of the company should be orchestrated to deliver the end service.

To create a positive team spirit, you need to be very clear about the company mission and the current strategy of your company, as it relates to your area of responsibility. Communicate continuously with your staff to be sure they understand the mission and current objectives.

The mission statement of the business should provide guidance about the principles on which you base your decisions. If the mission states, for example, "We provide excellent customer service", then that should be a foundation for your decisions. If your current strategic objective requires strict cost controls, then that should be evident in your decisions, too. The mission statement and strategic objectives are the source you use to define tasks and make decisions. Refer to these sources consistently to deliver your message, and to respond to questions about your decisions.

Creating a productive team spirit by leading with a common objective isn't just a good idea—it's a must. With a clear objective that serves the good of everyone involved, frequent communication about how the objectives will and are being achieved, and leadership that promotes the accepted principles and values, there is nothing that a group of people cannot achieve.

Manage Productivity

Good leaders are able to focus on managing the productivity of their staff, and accept that people function in different ways. It is important to disassociate your view of the value of the person from the value of their service. This is not an easy task, as we have all been labelling people as "good" or "bad" since childhood.

This mindset is very damaging, and if you apply it to the people in your organization, you will soon have a prejudicial list of "good" and "bad" people. Good leaders are aware of the different behaviours of their staff members, and they are able to look beyond any negative impressions, and work with their positive contributions.

The vast majority of people mean well, and they want their contributions to be valuable. It is best to go through life giving people the benefit of the doubt. The alternative is to be cynical, and continually looking for reasons to support the label you have applied.

We're not advocating giving the benefit of doubt to a menacing-looking stranger you might bump into in a dark street; we're talking about people you see for several hours a day, every day of the week for several years.

It can be frustrating when people continually make mistakes, regularly don't understand what is required, or always seem to need your attention—"high maintenance" people. We have all had to work with people who don't do things the way that we would do them, or prefer that they be done. If you are able to move beyond being critical about the person, and focus more on the service they provide, you will be able to be more objective and less likely to insult the person.

If you accept that there is more than one way to do the job, you will have a very constructive approach. Don't judge what people do by the label you have assigned to them. Be open to accepting that the way they perform a task may be different than your own approach, but it gets the job done. If, on the other hand, the worker's approach does not result in a satisfactory outcome, you can talk about what needs to be done so that, next time, you get what you want. If people don't understand what needs to be done, or they do understand, but don't have the ability, you must take action to improve the situation. Perhaps training or coaching will help, or perhaps they are in the wrong field of service. Whatever it takes, it's better to do something than to continually have to comment on poor performance, thereby reinforcing your labels.

Managing the objectives, rather than the personalities and the different ways people may go about completing their tasks, is how good leaders stay focused and productive. This also serves to limit negative personal comments that interfere with a positive environment.

Give Clear Directions to Reduce Resistance

It is essential that directions are clear, giving people the chance to perform their tasks independent of management involvement. Too often we see managers having to give constant guidance to their staff, not because the staff member isn't capable of completing the task alone, but because the manager did not provide clear directions at the outset. This situation can create frustration for the employee and the manager, both parties feeling a degree of inadequacy in each other. In addition, when a manager has a high need to control what people do, it can cause resistance. Controlling managers usually dole out directions on an as-needed basis. This leads to the staff feeling unsatisfied with their contribution, and with a negative opinion about their manager's behaviour.

When people have a clear understanding of what needs to be done and, if necessary, a specific process to complete a task in a certain way, they have what they need to perform. If a manager or supervisor allows people to complete their tasks without constant supervision, it creates an environment of trust. Over time, if people are confident that the tasks they are given will not be micro-managed, they are more likely to accept new tasks without resistance. An employee should reasonably expect to be asked for progress reports, and also to give evidence that the work has been completed. It is, after all, a key component of a manager's responsibility to distribute tasks, and ensure that they are completed in a timely manner, and with acceptable quality, as defined by the company.

Clearly defining objectives will not only make it easy for all parties to work together, it will also allow for the worker to move ahead alone. This can be very inspiring to the worker, and will ensure the manager has the time to focus on other productive activities.

Have the Desire to Help Others

The satisfaction of helping others develop their capabilities can become like an addiction, and can lead to significant and wonderful service to everyone with whom you come into contact. People who have a sincere desire to help others develop are easy to spot. They are generally happy and nearly always contribute beyond their direct areas of responsibility. They attract other people to them, because they make a positive difference to their environment.

New experiences and learning opportunities increase our capabilities. If you are able to provide opportunities to others to help them improve their capabilities, you will be well received. It is easy to recognize when you are giving useful help or advice. Typically, the recipients will be very open to your input, and you will see their energy level rise. Their speech rate may increase or their eyes widen. In most cases, they will show genuine gratitude for your help. Your sincere desire to help will create trust and loyalty that will go beyond the boundaries of your job description. People will attempt the impossible for a leader who has a genuine interest in helping them to develop their abilities.

If your genuine effort to help a colleague does not create the high-energy response you expect, it may be that your colleague has fallen into a rut, and forgotten what attracted him to the job in the first place. You may be giving him important advice that he would consider if he felt aligned with what he is doing. But if not, he is unlikely to gain any true satisfaction from the offer of help.

This may mean that your colleague should consider changing jobs; but that's not always the case. It might be better to help him rediscover the challenge in his current job.

Paul, the president of a business that employs about fifty fulltime staff, has an interesting philosophy: he accepts that he will sometimes lose a person to another company because the employee has developed their abilities beyond the role his company can provide.

This philosophy helps create a stimulating environment of talent development. It means there is a degree of turnover, and some discomfort when a good person leaves. But it creates an environment of growth that is beneficial to the staff and customers.

The alternatives are not very attractive: Paul could be satisfied with staff who have no interest in progressing in their abilities; he could limit a person's development, or have a person underachieving by operating below their capabilities. These will create both frustration and dissatisfaction in the workforce.

A leader's desire and ability to genuinely help develop staff and implement this philosophy throughout the organization has a direct influence on the company's ability to provide first class service to their customers. The returns for developing employees may not be as obvious a success measure as earnings per share, but a company will certainly be working less effectively if this critical component is ignored.

Meet Face-to-Face

A significant proportion of communication in today's global economy cannot be conducted face-to-face. While having some contact is better than having none, using telephone, e-mail, web chat, video conferencing or any of the social networking tools cannot deliver the same value as meeting in person can.

As we have already discussed in previous sections, the largest part of communication between two people is exchanged, not in the words, but by the tone and body language of the person delivering the message. While technology has allowed us to see people clearly through various meeting technologies, they do not yet allow projection of the emotions of a conversation as clearly as when meeting face-to-face. Also, what is said just prior to the official start or end of a meeting is often as valuable as the conversation during the meeting.

It is true that meeting in person usually takes longer than sending an e-mail or calling on the phone. But the return for the time invested by meeting in person can be significant, particularly as time goes by and the meeting time together accumulates to form the basis of a working relationship.

We are not suggesting that all other modes of communication should be avoided; that simply isn't practical or effective. But whenever there is a message of importance, and it is practical to meet with someone in person, or simply when it has been some time since you last met with someone, take the time to meet in person, if you can.

When leading people who are dispersed over a large office complex or in different geographical locations, take the time to meet with people and ensure that your staff feel connected to you and to each other. If an impersonal approach like e-mail is the only way your staff ever hears from you, it is highly unlikely that you will create the kind of strong bond that can make a material difference in achieving the company objectives. Everybody deserves to know that their contribution is valuable, and there is no better way of doing that than by having their group leader arriving to deliver a message in person.

We all work together to provide a service to others, and this does not only apply to our end customers. One of the ways we provide a service is by relating well with others within our company.

It may not be necessary to know the names of all of the family members of each of your staff members and what their personal interests are, but truly getting to know your staff does include having some level of knowledge about their lives outside of work. It isn't practical to get to know all of your staff members well when there are hundreds or thousands of people in your line of responsibility, but there is no excuse for being oblivious to the people that you interact with on a regular basis.

In our many years running companies and working with people who have leadership responsibilities, it never ceases to amaze us how many people don't follow the simple rule of meeting with co-workers, clients, and suppliers face to face. You may be surprised to hear that many leaders actively avoid meeting with people. Whether it is because they don't feel capable of talking effectively to their staff, or whether they (incredibly) think it is not necessary, too many leaders have not made meeting face-to-face with their staff a priority in their work.

There are many people who have reached significant levels of responsibility, but who fear meeting with people. If that is the case for you, we suggest you work with a coach to build your ability. It's rare that one has to do frequent public speaking engagements, and these opportunities require specific skills that can be taught. But being comfortable and effective in one on one or small group meetings will produce a significant advantage to achieving your objectives.

Leaders who take the time to get to know their staff put themselves in a position to receive valuable feedback. Some of the most valuable insights that leaders receive come from the informal times spent together; while meeting over dinner after all the business topics have been discussed, broader insights into the conditions of work will surface, and if the situation is right, more personal information may be shared. Respect for this information is critical. If you learn about circumstances through an informal situation, be very conscious of how you use that information. There's no quicker way to lose the respect of your staff than being caught spreading information that you received in confidence.

Remember, sharing doesn't mean intruding; a relationship based on respect doesn't include the need to pry. When people feel it is right to share some aspect of their personal life, they will.

When this happens, you should feel grateful that they are extending their trust to you.

Meeting people and holding discussions in person creates opportunities for multi-dimensional feedback. It serves to strengthen personal relationships, provides a sense of importance that all workers appreciate, and significantly increases your leadership effectiveness.

Motivate Your Staff

Motivating staff to deliver a desired objective is another key skill for getting great performance. People who have a purpose to achieve have a much better chance of success than those who are just going through the motions. Motivating people isn't about jumping up and down waving banners, making colourful speeches, or promising the earth. These kinds of actions usually have a short-term influence.

The key to motivating people is to be sincere, and to have a clear and valuable objective that serves the broader community. You need to communicate the message in a way that it is easily understood and shows how achievement of the objective will benefit all involved. The ability to deliver a message that really resonates with your staff and creates a confident "will do" environment is an ability that is worth investing in.

Sometimes the objective is not an attractive prospect; maybe you have to reorganize by downsizing your department, and there will be casualties. Even this depressing news, if accompanied by a clear statement of direction, can be presented in a motivating way.

Consider the meaning of the word "motivate". Motivation is more than just making others feel great about a target, and moving towards it. Motivation is a way of communicating, in a persuasive manner, the reason to move in a certain direction. It's great when the motivation is to win a trip to Hawaii, but real life isn't always about pleasant things. Sometimes we have to motivate people through the tough stuff, too.

When Sarah joined a new company as VP of Sales, her first task was to do a deep evaluation of the business and establish some early objectives. The business had been running at a loss over the last two years, and revenue had not shown any growth for several years. The economy wasn't very conducive to growth, and to the outsider, that might be sufficient excuse for the lacklustre performance. But when Sarah started looking, it didn't take much digging to learn the real cause.

There was great focus on the customer experience, which was positive, but there was little focus or discipline applied to the administration of the business. There was a relaxed atmosphere, and people appeared happy to work in the office. But this proved to be a negative indicator. People were happy at work because they had no accountability. Targets were set, but staff continued to receive their full variable pay, even when the targets were not achieved. Sarah had her work cut out for her, but she was not put off by a bit of hard work.

The first thing Sarah did was to realign compensation to company objectives. The company couldn't continue to pay out bonuses when company targets had not been met. The processes to deliver product to their customers was good, but processes to sustain the business were not. Sarah's biggest concern was how the sales team would react to the changes.

Sarah recalls one particularly important meeting. She had to motivate the sales team to accept a new order, to become energetic, goal-oriented, and more productive. The alternative was too bleak to contemplate. The company was closer to being out of business than many people realized, mostly because the current happy, relaxed approach was masking the fact that their business was in trouble.

Sarah called all of the sales people into the boardroom. She started off with the bleak news. "This ship is sinking, and if we don't fix the leaks and chart a new course fast, we will go down." The team was shocked. They all liked working there, and the thought of losing their jobs was distressing. Sarah continued, "I know how we can turn this around, and I will tell you what we need to do, but it will require commitment from all of you." The team was now nervous, wondering what uncomfortable situation they were about to find themselves in.

"First, variable compensation will now be directly linked to individual performance; there will be no more team pay. The days of the company paying on-target commissions for under performance is history."

Of course, this created a murmur and some flushed faces; it sounded a lot like accountability. Sarah continued, "I have studied what we do, and how long tasks take. I accept that, as a sales team we do too much administration, so many admin tasks will be redirected. This will help us with the next objective. Effective immediately, your sales activity rates will increase from 25 contacts per day to 40 contacts per day.

The sky had fallen. Disagreements came thick and fast, but Sarah held on. Sarah reiterated some of her opening statements, and continued to acknowledge that it would not be easy. But the truth was that they could follow her path, or consider that they would all be looking for new employment before long.

Sarah continued, "I can save you some pain now, if you prefer. Anyone who does not want to follow this new direction can leave now."

This was clearly a very bold statement, but the time for sugarcoating the realities had passed. However, there was a bright light as Sarah wrapped up the meeting. "I believe in this team, and I believe our company provides a great service. We can make our company strong and sustainable. It will take hard work, but we will have fun in the process. I am committed to taking this company to a place where we can all be proud of our achievements, and I want all of you to come with me."

Following up, we can tell you that the team did increase their activity rates to 40 contacts per day, and then a few months later, to 50.

Commissions were linked to individual performance, but it didn't take long before the sales people earned more than they had previously. Some of the most innovative sales programs came out of Sarah's team, and it went on to become an example for the other sales divisions in the company to follow.

It wasn't all smooth sailing, but the course had been set. Sarah had motivated the sales team with her message. It was delivered with sincerity, and she presented a clearly stated objective with practical implementation, all for the good of the broader community.

Balance the Value of People and Process

Having measurable processes that lead your business toward its objectives will enhance your chances of success. Having the right people with appropriate skills, trained for their tasks, and aware of their objectives will also improve your chances of success. However, the right people with poor processes, or great processes being performed poorly are both likely to produce poor outcomes.

Processes that become over-developed and dominate the workplace need to be pruned. If this is not done, the processes can become the source of overworked people performing largely irrelevant tasks. And too much conformity can lead to people becoming robotic. Opportunities to improve the business may be overlooked. People who become complacent need to be reminded of their objectives and purpose in the business. People who are well-trained, but find their creativity stifled by over-built processes will become disenchanted.

Generating significant company growth usually requires a degree of creativity. Likewise, for a person to be able to grow, they must be able to put creative ideas into action. Too much creativity, on the other hand, can lead to a chaotic environment in which it is difficult to define how to achieve what you want, and how you arrived at what you achieved. A balance needs to be maintained, and that balance is dependent on the type of business you are running. Some environments require strict conscious obedience to process, for example, in a hospital. Some environments require ongoing creativity, for example, marketing a product. All business environments need both process and creativity, but the balance should be tailored to the business requirements.

The balance along the continuum of conformity and creativity will sometimes slide toward one end or the other. To define when and where creativity can be expressed in your business, you need to know the required balance. If your processes are well-tuned, the safe route is to rely on them. Isolating creative concepts and testing them before integrating them into your system allows you to stay true to your processes, while managing creativity. If you are in a conservative environment, it is good to be open to a creative burst of action every now and again—this will stir the pot, and can lead to some fun and beneficial experiences.

Be aware of your company's needs for process and creativity. All process and no creativity can lead to a dull work environment. However, the primary objective is to provide a valuable service to your customers, so don't forsake that objective, if you find that too much creativity causes chaos. Continually review where your business is on the creativity-conformity continuum to be sure you are not limiting your progress with either overly rigid or overly flexible processes.

Qualify All Sides of Conflicts

Conflict management is a very sensitive subject. Probably the best and easiest rule to follow is this: don't jump to conclusions, and be sure to listen to both sides of a conflict before giving your opinions to either side.

Conflicts generally fall into three categories. The first category, and the easiest to deal with, is a lack of information. This is often resolved by good communication.

The second category of conflict involves a difference in values. This provides a greater challenge, as each side must be able to acknowledge and respect the other's point of view. The solution may require a combination of both perspectives.

The most challenging category of conflict involves personalities and previous differences between the two parties. This type of conflict will call on your highest level of skill as a leader because, if these people are required to continue to work together, they must be able to resolve their differences and leave them behind.

Most of the conflicts that will be brought to your attention will be rooted in values and personalities. The most common situation will involve a person raising an issue, and then asking you not to repeat anything of your discussion to the other party. In this case you must make it clear that if you can't talk about the issue with the other party, then your role will be limited to being a sounding board.

In this situation, be careful not to be critical of the other party. You also shouldn't be overly sympathetic with the person who has brought the complaint; this will serve only to support their convictions. Keep in mind that your agreement, although meant in a passive supportive way, can be used against you later. You must make a decision immediately whether you are prepared to be only a sounding board, since once you have stated this intention, you must not renege on your promise.

If the case brought forward has implications beyond hurt feelings, then you will have to stand up to the situation, and tell the complainant that you cannot limit yourself to providing a sounding board; not addressing it with the other party will cause more harm than good.

The decision to bring the opposing parties together in the same room must be made on a case-by-case basis. Sometimes airing views together with you as the mediator can work, and sometimes it can backfire. When listening to either side give their opinion, it is important to listen and, as appropriate, check that you have the correct understanding. Be sure not to agree to one position before you have all the information, as that may rebound on you if the other party has an even more convincing position. Let it be known at the outset that you will listen to all parties involved before taking any action, or even expressing an opinion.

If a situation seems to be going around in circles, if it is dragging on, or if one position is clearly unacceptable, then as the senior person involved, you must make a decision. In this case, being clear with your reasoning and applying consistent values will help. The "loser" in the affair probably won't agree with your decision, but the hope is that a mature attitude will prevail. Not making a decision in these cases, or flip-flopping in favour of one side and then the other, can be like planting a seed of negativity. Not only will the disagreeing parties continue with their argument, probably escalating it, your handling of the situation will also become an issue and you could lose the respect of your staff.

In conflict management, tough decisions have to be made. There may not be obvious cost implications, but having disgruntled staff members can be an invisible cost that, if it were visible on a balance sheet, would be frightening.

Remain consistent to your values, try to separate the personalities from the issues, and take action as quickly you can.

Give Sweet and Sour Feedback Appropriately

There are few things in life that are sweeter than receiving recognition for a job well done in front of friends and colleagues. Equally, there are few things as sour as being chastised in front of friends and colleagues. Giving sincere praise in public, and saving the criticism for delivery in private, is a good general rule to apply.

We recommend that you consider everyone you work with as your customer, in one form or another. The service they provide is either directly or indirectly linked to your own performance. If you berate a person in public, it is hardly likely to motivate them to work harder; therefore your actions will at some level have an impact on your own performance. In addition, those who watch you dress down another will make a mental note about your behaviour, and it won't be a favourable one even if they do appear to accept or agree with your criticism.

John was the manager of a small team of people. He made a conscious effort to praise people in public. He made a point of looking for evidence that people in his team had done well, and when he found it, he immediately went to the person's work space to commend them. He specifically identified what had been done well, and thanked the person for their contribution. This became a regular habit for John, and he soon found that he was seeing good things happen all over the place. Maybe they had always been happening, and John hadn't noticed, or possibly his frequent praise to the staff had increased their performance levels—it was probably a bit of both. John found that, once he had developed the habit of noticing the good things that his team had produced, he would find good things happening everywhere; in other departments, at home, everywhere he looked.

John didn't confine his praise to just his own staff; the reaction he got from them was just too delightful. Soon John found great satisfaction in praising everyone who did something beyond normal expectations. It is amazing how, when you start looking for the good stuff, it shows up everywhere!

Of course, life isn't a bed of roses. John had his fair share of under-performance to deal with, too. Whenever sour feedback was required, he would arrange to meet the person in his office, and close the door for privacy. As with the praise, John was always specific and timely with any critical comments he had to dispense. Rather than taking the power position behind his large desk, John would sit at a round table with the employee. This would lead to a more open and constructive conversation. After all, the objective was not to make the employee feel like a scolded child. The conversation would focus on the issue, what caused the below-par performance, and what the employee needed to do to ensure better performance in the future.

After the meeting, the employee would be clear on what needed to change, but without feeling inadequate or insulted.

John had created an environment where the employees did not feel belittled when receiving critical feedback. The staff was not afraid to make mistakes. The team had an acceptable format in which poor performance could be discussed; they knew what was expected of them. When they did well, they were praised, when they didn't do well, they were told about that, too. Nothing was swept under the carpet, and at employee performance time, there were never any surprises.

John understood that making sure the team always knew what their goals were, as well as being told frequently what was done very well and what was not acceptable, played an important role in their success.

Understand the Impact of Negativity

A negative attitude in the office can spread like a virus, and can kill productivity in the environment. Negative people are easy to spot; they are always complaining about everything and everyone. Usually they don't voice their concerns in a constructive manner, or even to anyone who can address the issues. They are not looking to improve the environment with their complaints; complaining is just what they do.

Sadly for negative people, it is not the environment that causes their condition. Wherever they show up, whatever the occasion, they can be counted on to have a negative opinion about something.

Complaining, or disagreeing with something that is happening is not, in itself, negative. It is healthy to hear different perspectives, especially opposing opinions, as they can generate constructive discussion. But it crosses the line when a particular person is always complaining, and when they do not contribute any suggestions for improving the situation.

If your workplace has a negative atmosphere, your leadership ability will be severely challenged until you can turn it around. Regardless of how mundane a job may be, no job is negative. There are only people who have negative attitudes. There is a balance of power that negativity seeks to reach. If one negative attitude can successfully infect another person, and then another, eventually you will have more negative people in the office than those who are neutral or positive.

This is a dangerous position to be in. The positive people are likely to find the environment unacceptable, and look elsewhere for work, and because positive people are usually more productive, the output of the office will be negatively affected. New people coming in to the office will quickly understand the situation; they will then either join the negative bunch, or decide to do what they can despite the atmosphere. In any event, managing a team with a pervasive negative atmosphere is no fun at all. You will be trudging uphill every day just to get the bare minimum objectives completed.

Negativity generally resides in the HMw (Human Middleware). This is conditioning that can be reprogrammed. As we have outlined in this book, recognizing our conditioning and reprogramming our HMw for success is essential, but it is also very personal. It is not something another person can do for you. In other words, you cannot change the negative attitude of other people; they have to want to change it for themselves. If you motivate the desire for people to reprogram their HMw then you might be able to provide the guidance that could change their lives for the better. If they are not willing to grow and develop, then the path becomes tougher for all concerned.

However you handle the situation, understand that you cannot have a fully-functioning business with negative attitudes in the group.

The last resort is to remove the person with the negative attitude. The degree to which you have the time, patience, and willingness to work with the negative person will define how much you are prepared to do before either the person understands that their attitude is a problem and is willing to change, or you remove them.

The decision to remove a person should not be taken lightly, but as described above, you cannot afford to let the negativity disease spread. It is particularly difficult to justify removing a top performer who is negative. This isn't a common occurrence as negative people aren't usually top performers, but it does happen. At some point, you will have to bite the bullet; the performance of one person rarely overshadows the performance of many. Without the negative high performer, it is likely that the others in the group will become more productive.

Sometimes, the negative person appears to be popular and this might be an obstacle that affects how you resolve the issue. You know that whatever you try to do with the person, it will be spun out of context, and circulated among your people, because that is what complainers do. Don't be fooled by what appears to be popularity. Often people give time to the complainers just to be sure they haven't become the object of gossip. We have witnessed occasions when a "popular" complainer was removed from a department, and the collective sigh of relief was almost audible. Productivity immediately improved.

By removing negative attitudes, you will create a better, more productive environment, and people will respect you for your actions.

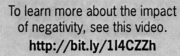 To learn more about the impact of negativity, see this video.
http://bit.ly/1I4CZZh

Set Beneficial Targets

There are few tasks that are as potentially volatile as the setting of compensation-based targets. If set well, they can be very constructive. If the staff considers them unfair or too complex they can be very destructive. Compensation-based targets have a variable income component such as a commission plan or a short term event bonus. To be generally accepted, variable income-based targets should be well-defined from the beginning, and they should be realistic, easy to track, and set up to motivate people toward a clearly stated goal.

Equally important—incentive plans should be targeted for achieving an important company objective. Too often, annual incentive plans are left static for a number of years, and eventually the company requirements are not driving the mechanism for payments.

Variable income targets are typically based on projections. While it might be easy to define the company objectives, it is often more luck than judgement to accurately project a fair payment structure. For annual plans, being generally consistent from year to year in the methods you use to calculate variable pay will help your people understand what they need to do.

> *"Targets that don't build people up might wear them down."*

For example; the calculation methods and payment value of the components can be consistent, even when the actual components targeted are changed. Broad changes on an annual basis can leave people feeling confused about the company direction, and sceptical about the intentions of the plan.

Don't change the plan mid-term even if your plan is under-paying, and you want to change it to create a better chance to achieve. While your intentions are honourable, it might set a precedent that will be counterproductive later.

Changing a plan mid-term because it is paying more than you expected will result in serious complaints, and may also contravene employment rules. If it turns out that you have significantly miscalculated your projections, and despite their hard work, no one is near target, you can consider adding a discretionary bonus plan. This will meet the objective by continuing to incentivise productivity, but will not compromise the integrity of the previously defined plan.

That doesn't mean that if the economy or some other external factor seriously impacts the productivity of your business that you should still pay out; that is not a win-win situation and you should ensure your people understand the difficult conditions.

The plan should be straightforward enough for employees on the plan to calculate their current payment projection; this will allow them to stay involved with their progress. Any incentive plan worth having is always well tracked. If your people don't know or don't care what their current incentive plan is projected to pay, it's not much of an incentive. If the method to calculate the incentive is complex or requires statistics that are not available to the person on the payment plan, the key motivating element will be lost—the employee can no longer calculate what he needs do to increase the value. For short term incentives, particularly if an incentive has a team component, having a large illustration on the wall as a reminder of the current status, shows people where they are, and should add momentum to the incentive.

A variable component of pay can be an extremely good motivating tool for a leader to use. Be fair, consistent, and willing to explain how you arrived at your plan. If you have made an honest mistake in your projections, admit it and explain; employees will understand. Providing that you are open to fixing problems so that the plan meets the needs of the company and the staff, you should be on safe ground.

A well thought-out variable income plan that is easy for the employees to track can accelerate the achievement of company objectives creating a win-win environment for the employees and the company.

LEADING PEOPLE SUMMARY

Leading People involves motivating others and managing what they do. After mastering these abilities, you have the power to affect people's lives in both positive and negative ways.

Below is the chart highlighting the abilities presented in this section, followed by the positive behaviours that characterize them. The negative behaviours described in the last column are those that appear when these leadership abilities are not present.

Abilities	Positive Behaviours	Negative Behaviours
Hires well	New hires fit well	High turnover and poor take-up rate
Creates team spirit	Facilitates common direction	Creates and allows chaos
Manages productivity	Focuses on action rather than personalities	Critical and judgemental
Gives directions that reduce resistance	Gives clear directions	Creates confusion; micromanages
Wants to help others	Has others in mind; gives praise	Selfish; doesn't recognize others' contributions
Meets face-to-face	Gets multi-dimensional feedback and builds strong relationships	Doesn't know what's going on; does not build strong relationships
Motivates staff	Charges people up, provides clear objectives	Assumes people will do what they are told
Balances value of people and process	Good balance between creativity and conformity	Is either too creative (chaos) or too formal

Abilities	Positive Behaviours	Negative Behaviours
Qualifies all sides of the conflicts	Supportive yet neutral; unafraid to make tough decisions	Takes sides; breaches confidences
Gives sweet and sour feedback appropriately	Praises in public, admonishes in private	Belittles publicly
Understands the impact of negativity	Deals with negative issues	Allows gossip and backstabbing
Sets beneficial targets appropriately	Sets plans that motivate	People complain and feel cheated

LEADING BUSINESS

A good business leader adds incremental value to their business beyond expected performance. This means that in growth times, your business grows faster than expected, or as compared to similar businesses. In difficult times when the business is declining, you are able to minimize the pain, as compared to expectations, or as compared to similar businesses. Many abilities come into play for good performance as a business leader. How you lead people is a very important factor, as we discussed earlier. Knowing your business and the market intimately is the basis from which you will be able to navigate your business through calm and stormy conditions.

As we discussed in the Leading People section, your leadership style is important; this is also true for leading your business. Your style is largely defined by how hands-on you are in your business. Being hands-on doesn't necessarily mean micro-managing, but standing too far back from the business can be as bad as standing too close.

Being organized is another requirement for leading a business and there are several definitions of, and methodologies for, being organized.

Your openness to sharing information with others is also a factor that will define your business leadership style.

Taking care of how your business runs is a key component of leading a business. It can take a long time to get a really good grip on how the business is run. It is absolutely necessary to take the time required to understand it completely. After a business is running well, it is much easier to continue along the path already defined, and only make changes as needs determine.

The alternative is to lead your business on an undefined or ad hoc basis, but having to continually respond to the market's ups and downs will put you on the defensive. And if this condition lasts for long, it will be chaotic. Chaos is generally considered an inferior style of leadership and will likely compound any other issues that you have to face.

Know the Business in Data Terms

When your value to the business has gone beyond completing tasks and involves leading people and implementing strategy, you will need a thorough understanding of all the statistical indicators related to your company. Speaking competently with people from different departments requires that you know how their departments relate and contribute to the larger organizational objectives. Understanding their key responsibilities and recognizing what their challenges are will give you a great advantage when communicating with them.

In the same way that a person might keep track of key health indicators like weight, blood pressure, or cholesterol levels, it is beneficial to know and track the key indicators in your company. The key indicators alone don't tell you why things are happening the way they are, but they give you numerical results about how the various aspects of the company are doing. Reviewing key data will keep you aware of what is going on, and if the data worries you, you can then choose to find out the cause of the poor indicators.

In some organizations, there is a lot of data; the trick is finding what is useful. In other organizations, there is almost no data available. Whatever your level of responsibility, your first task in gathering data is to define what the important aspects of your business are. Your own area of responsibility will have metrics by which it is measured. You should also identify what data you need on a broader basis. The goal here is to give you a broader perspective of your organization, and also to prepare you for when you are offered more responsibility. Once you have made a list, you can then go in search of the data that matches your needs. If the data is not available, then authorize the collection of the data or speak to someone who can.

Once you have organized the delivery of the data to you on a regular basis, analyze it thoroughly. This is particularly important at the outset as you make yourself familiar with the data. After a while you will hone in on the specific statistics most relevant to you.

As well as understanding the data and gaining broader, dynamic business knowledge, your key objective is to be able to recognize subtle changes when they occur. Often you will find signals of what might be coming to your business. The data can give you an early indicator of changes that are not yet large enough to see in the workforce. Waiting until the changes are large enough to see at a macro level may result in harmful effects that require critical attention.

Knowing your business in data terms will give you a very real advantage in leading your business. While a snapshot of data won't give you immediate answers, over a short period of time reviewing data, consistently gathered, will inspire questions.

Many great ideas have been hatched, and many calamities have been avoided, by paying close attention to business data. If you can see the future, and solve problems before they have time to gain momentum, you will gain a great deal of credibility, and opportunities will come to you.

Be Informed

The difference between being informed, and understanding the data, is the source. Data, as we have discussed, is presented in report form, and shows you results. The information you need comes from your people, and will give you important insights about why and how things are occurring.

With the responsibility of leading in business, it becomes important to make the time required to be informed about what is occurring throughout the business. If you have a heavy workload, it can become a challenge to keep up with all that is going on in your own department, let alone what is happening in other places. If this is the case for you, be aware that this is a red flag indicating that something of importance may blindside you and cause significant discomfort.

You must remember that information gathering time is not the time to interfere. Unless it is urgent, it is better not to make judgements on what is occurring during your regular check-up process.

For example; if every time you ask a person how this or that is progressing and you always manage to find an issue, you are less likely to get the full story in the future. Instead, collect your information and assess it before you decide to inquire further or make decisions about changes.

We recommend that you set up both a formal process and an informal process for staying informed. The formal process should centre on meetings with specific people to learn what is happening. The meeting is for your benefit, and you should make it clear that the objective is for you to learn. It is OK to include time for the person you are meeting with to ask questions, but you should not get distracted from your objective; if you do, you will find your routine update meetings will lose their importance. If you find it beneficial to have two or three participants because their responsibilities overlap, that is fine. But be sure to keep control of the meeting; and your objective.

The informal process is just as important. Make the effort to walk the office or workplace as often as you can. Speak to different people about what they are doing, and what issues they face. It is amazing how often critical issues can be addressed in the early stages by the impromptu information you get when on a walk-about.

The habit of consistently maintaining up-to-date knowledge of what is happening in your business will contribute to your ability to make sound decisions. It will also help you avoid bigger issues down the road. When people know that you are curious about the business, and you are making an effort to keep up to date without making judgements, they will make the effort to ensure that you are kept in the loop.

See the Complete Picture

Understanding the mission of your business and the current strategic objectives is important for you to be able to make an effective contribution. If your organization is headed east, and your contributions are facing west, then you are more likely to develop and propose ideas that will not be accepted. Worse still, you could invest time and resources only to confuse everyone. Keeping up to date with news about your industry, how the economy is affecting your business and listening to senior management updates should give you enough insight to know at least the general direction the business is travelling.

Remember that the collective objective of a company is to be sustainable while serving as many customers as possible. Keep a close watch on new services, product releases, and revisions. What do they tell you about the market you are serving?

Alison was a very competitive and growth-driven person. She was the manager of a business line, and she was always thinking about ways to expand her contribution. While in a managers' meeting listening to a senior manager presentation, her interest was piqued; she heard that the products in her business line were about to be increased. Alison was thrilled and her mind immediately started to consider many different ways that she could market a larger product line.

After the meeting had concluded, Alison went to the President's office. She explained how excited she was at hearing that her product line was to be expanded. She continued to say that with the right plan and great execution, there was a real opportunity that her business line could become the fastest growing part of the company, and maybe even become the catalyst of significant overall growth for the business.

Allison was sure this kind of message would be well-received. But she didn't get the response she was expecting. The President described his plan for running the business; his plan was very controlled and cautious. The idea of running full speed ahead into a very competitive market could have a negative impact on the company. There was a chance that the core business might suffer, and the decision to expand the product line would come back to bite them.

He told Allison that he wanted a slow and controlled approach to developing her business line; he wanted the company to test every new step to ensure a high degree of confidence that the desired outcomes would be achieved.

Although this response may seem negative to some people, others will understand it, and for Alison, it was an important lesson. Her excited initial thoughts were not wrong, but before taking any decisive action, it was important to understand the complete picture.

To Alison's credit, she was neither offended nor discouraged by the president's remarks, and she thanked him for his insight. Alison understood that when she went back to her business unit, she would now be better able to create effective plans for her team; plans that would be congruent with the company objectives, and less likely to cause a disturbance.

It is important to understand the strategic direction of your company if you are to play an effective role in its broader objectives. Your company may be in expansion mode, whether organic or through acquisition. Your company may be in a contracting mode. Maybe the economy has had a punishing effect, and you are witnessing cost and headcount reductions. Perhaps your company is run using a very cautious and conservative approach, and new ideas need to be contained. Since there are many possible strategic directions, it is important for you to see the complete picture before implementing your decisions.

Be Organized

Being organized isn't just about having tidy piles of paper on your desk, or having multiple project-based folders in your e-mail client. Organization is a state of mind. The tidy environments that people maintain are an outward manifestation of their inner organized mind. There are numerous creative and practical benefits that accrue from being organized.

To be organized, you need to have a clear purpose. If you have a purpose for your day, a particular meeting, or a larger business objective, it is easy to set parameters. Knowing what you want to achieve will make it easy for you to recognize when you have achieved it. This can be very motivating, since when you reach the end of a task, you can tick it off your list. Remember to reward yourself in some way as you complete your major milestones, as this will reinforce your habit of being organized.

Disorganization can lead to stress, which is how you feel when you're out of control. When it seems there are too many things to do, and not enough time or resources to do them, it can be very stressful. Being organized will help you to keep things in perspective, and will reduce your feelings of stress.

Writing a list enables you to evaluate what tasks actually need to be completed, and which are just cluttering your mind. Keeping a list of tasks to be done is the first step toward controlling stress; applying a priority to each task is the next step.

Brad was a hard-working, conscientious worker. He was quite organized, and kept his task list updated. One month, feeling overwhelmed by the amount of work he had to do, Brad decided to review his task list with his manager. It was long, about five pages of bullet points. When Brad described it, his manager realized that the long list was creating stress. Reviewing the list, Brad's manager recognized a few tasks that he thought were old. When he asked Brad what type of priority he had applied to the list, Brad's answer was, "None". As he had learned about new tasks, Brad had simply added them to his list.

Brad's manager suggested he review the list and create a priority coding. Brad did this, and the next time they met, Brad showed his revised list to his manager. It looked a lot less daunting. There were still many outstanding tasks, but only a few were high priority. There were still a number of things that Brad could do to manage his list better, but organizing it by priority significantly reduced his stress levels.

Another aspect of being organized is taking a few moments to organize your thoughts, and make a few notes before an event or meeting. This can make you far more efficient in the meeting.

Consider all the points you think are important, and set the order in which you want to cover them. Consider the responses you are likely to receive. Often, we assume that the responses will be in our favour. But what if you get a totally unexpected response? Will you be caught off guard?

Being prepared for an unexpected response served John, a business leader, well. When John was distributing incentive plans to his managers, he thought he was on safe ground. The plans were similar to the previous year's plans, and if anything they seemed more achievable. He thought the presentation would be a quick meeting, and everyone would go away happy. But that didn't happen. One manager felt it was time for change, and presented his opinion in a very emotional way. This scenario could have quickly spun out of control. Fortunately, John was organized and had taken time before the meeting to prepare a response in the event of a disagreement. Of course, there is no way you can consider every possible objection, but even being prepared for the possibility of an objection is very useful. Instead of feeling over-confident, John was not taken by surprise and was able to discuss the issues raised.

The practical aspect of being organized is that it makes you more efficient. If you always have large disorganized piles of papers strewn across your desk, even if you think you can lay your hands on what you need when you need it, you do increase the risk of missing something. When people come into your office and see the state of your desk, it will give them the impression that you are a messy person. Some people just get too much paper work to realistically expect to have a clean desk top, while others find it calming to work among piles of paper. We suggest that you ask yourself honestly whether your organization system is helping or hindering you, and whether your "system" is truly a system, or just random.

Being organized isn't just a technique you can apply to accelerate your career. It is a lifestyle choice that will pay benefits in all areas of home and work life. It can take a while to become organized in all areas of your business, but once you have, you will find it is quite easy to maintain. Reducing stress, being prepared, knowing where things are, and developing your business, are just a few of the benefits you will experience if you take control and organize your mind and your environment.

Lead from the Front and from the Rear

Leading a business does not mean you have to lead every task. On the contrary, often leading requires that you let others take the controls. You did not get to a level of leadership because you were the best at doing everything. You have strong skills and refined abilities, but you also know that some things require skills that you don't have. In fact, the truth is, most things require skills you don't have. Don't worry; this isn't an insult, just reality. You need to focus on being the best leader you can be, which mostly means getting the best out of the talented people around you.

When you understand that leadership is about allowing and helping other people do what they are good at, you will have taken a significant step toward earning more, and a broader set of, responsibilities.

When David ran a business that had offices in a downtown location, his business suffered a flood. All of the company computers that were shipped for use at customer sites were stored in the basement of the building. When the flood occurred, the contents of the basement were in jeopardy of being severely damaged. When David got the call advising him that the basement was being flooded, he rushed downstairs to see how bad things were.

When he got there he saw that one of his managers had assumed control of the situation. People were being directed and tasks were quickly being assigned. As David was the business leader, people naturally turned to him for instructions. In fact, David was not the best at giving instructions for this type of emergency situation, and he recognized the talent of the manager who had assumed control. David's most important role in this scenario was to make it clear that the manager was in control and assignments were to be taken from him. The flood action lasted for most of the day, and at the end, the damage was very limited. Had David felt the need to take control and lead the emergency effort, the outcome would not have been as good. The manager who did take the lead received the praise he deserved, and felt the pride of being able to lead even in the presence of a more senior person.

Leadership means facilitating the best outcome to a situation. It doesn't mean that you are the best at doing everything, or that people should follow only what you say and do. In most cases, leadership requires careful consideration of the various options. When it comes to reacting to emergency situations, don't assume that you must make all the decisions. Assess who is in the best position to respond, and give them the authority to lead. There are times to lead from the front and there are times to lead from the rear. Good leaders know the best way to lead for the various situations.

Apply a Decision-Making Process

People who frequently make sound decisions will gain the confidence of everyone they work with. To make sound decisions, you need a process.

Be consistent, apply your values and principles to all of your decisions, understand all of the facts, and work through all of the possible upside and downside outcomes. By following these steps, you will find it easier to make decisions that produce the desired outcomes.

Consistency is often more important to people than what you actually decide. Many of your daily decisions are minor, and may affect only a few people. Regardless of the impact of the decision, consistency should always be a priority.

If you have no standards on which you base your decisions, you will probably be unpredictable and confusing, and you may tend to take longer coming to a conclusion. Your business success will depend on your current mood, and that is not a good way to develop your career. However, if your decisions are based on a reasoned approach, even those who disagree with your decision will at least understand why you decided as you did.

When you are faced with a decision, and after you are in possession of all the supporting data, then you can contemplate your decision. Of course, you won't always have all the information that you would like, but at some point, waiting for more information will result in diminishing returns.

When considering the upside, you will often consider projected metrics, historic comparisons, opinions, and optimism. If there is no downside to the new plan and the cost of an action is acceptable, the decision is easy to make.

However, it is important to also understand the potential down side. Generally speaking, if you recognize the downside, you will have a better understanding of the risk involved, and be less likely to be taken in by the optimism of the upside potential. The downside can usually be accurately defined. A downside outcome could be the monetary cost of the action and the resources used.

The decision to go one way rather than another could result in a loss of market share, reduced quality of your product, or the loss of a key employee. All of these will be on your list of possible downside outcomes, and must be factored into your decision making process.

Christie, in her position as Sales Director, often acted like a bank manager. When sales people or sales managers brought new ideas for things they wanted to try, she would put on her bank manager hat and ask, "How much will it cost, what's the risk, and what do you expect to get in return?" If the sales manager bringing the ideas could not answer the questions, she would say "No", and send them away to do their homework.

This shouldn't be confused with paralysis by analysis; none of us has a crystal ball that can definitively tell us what the outcome of any decision will be. Too often, however, projects or campaigns are undertaken without a simple understanding of what the upside and downside could be. This may be driven by the desire and optimism of the project owner, who can only see the wonderful upside of his idea.

In that case, we hope the company has a level-headed "Christie" to apply her bank manager philosophy before moving forward.

Being consistent by applying your values and principles to your business decisions, having all the facts available, and applying the upside/downside rule will result in better decisions. After people understand your approach, and recognize the consistency in your decisions, you will find yourself explaining your decisions less and less often.

Have Productive Meetings

A well-organized meeting can be extremely valuable and productive. To ensure that you are on the right path, ask yourself whether a meeting is the best way to move toward your objective. Asking this question could save you and others countless hours. How many times have you attended a meeting and thought, "That's another hour I won't get back"?

Too many meetings do not begin with a clear and meaningful objective, and too often, participants leave empty-handed. In some environments, meetings may be so inefficient that the participants actually expect the time to be wasted.

Let's look at some ways that you can be sure that your meetings are relevant, and that attendees arrive with a view to learning something new, or contributing to the development of the business.

Have a purpose. If you are calling the meeting, be sure that you and the participants all have a clear understanding of what the purpose is. Knowing ahead of time will enable everyone to be as prepared as possible, and ready to contribute to the purpose. If there are any relevant materials, be sure to distribute them beforehand. If you are a participant and did not call the meeting, go with the intent to learn or contribute something. If you are not aware of the purpose of the meeting before hand, don't go in blind; ask what the meeting is meant to accomplish. If the subject does not appear to be relevant to you, don't go. If you are required to attend, look for the opportunity to learn.

Whether or not the subject of the meeting is relevant to you, don't waste your time by tuning out and working on your laptop or PDA. This is not only disrespectful and distracting for the speaker, but is also damaging to your reputation.

When you are leading a meeting, start by reconfirming the objective and the time allotted. Meetings of indeterminate length cause people to tune out. If the participants have a role to play, ask them at the beginning whether they all have the information they need to contribute. If you have handouts, make sure that everyone has what they should have. Realize that as soon as you hand out materials, people will review them. Only hand out what you need to, consider holding back any material that is not relevant until later in the meeting. You may also choose to hold back any information that could reduce the impact of your presentation.

Seating arrangements are not very important, but be aware that if you take the chair at the head of the table, you are now in a dominant position. If that is what you want, so be it. If you don't need it, then seating yourself in the centre of one side is likely to create a more inclusive environment. If you will need to frequently stand and move around the room, then your seating should be in a practical position. If there is any technological equipment involved, such as microphones or cameras, these should also be considered in your choice of seats.

If you want people to take notes, tell them when you open the meeting. It is preferable, though, to provide notes after the meeting. It can be distracting to participants to take notes while keeping up with the presentation. Having said that, ask your participants to make a note of any questions they have, if they cannot be asked immediately. If a person is trying to remember a question they are likely to miss the content presented until after they can speak.

Action items that come out of the meeting should be clearly stated in terms of what the action is, and most important, why the action should be completed. Responsibility should be applied to a person along with agreed completion times, resources available, and any other material aspects of the action item. Frequently, action items from meetings, particularly if there are too many, have a tendency to drift away, and are lost. Make sure people know that you will be following up on their progress. Unless the purpose of the meeting is purely information sharing, action items should be generated, but do not bombard the participants with action items. One or two action items per person should be sufficient.

Try to complete the meeting on time. If you can see that you are likely to go overtime, ask whether that is acceptable to the participants. If it is not acceptable, you will either have to continue without those who have to leave, or schedule a follow up meeting to complete the agenda. In any event, whether you are closing the meeting having completed all or only part of the agenda, be sure to summarize the meeting. This need only take a few minutes but it should include a list of action items and the person responsible for each one. Always leave more time for each item on the agenda than you think is necessary, this will allow for questions from the participants, or for additional explanations needed. You will never be seen in a poor light if your meeting finishes earlier than anticipated; this is usually received like a gift of additional time for the participants.

Every productive meeting concludes with a follow-up on actions items delegated. This is often a key item that is missed. If you don't follow-up, the actions probably won't happen.

After a meeting, it is a good practice to send out a message confirming the key points to the participants. Asking for feedback about the meeting process is a nice touch. This will give you confirmation of a good meeting, and possibly, tips for future meetings.

A well-run meeting can be a valuable use of resources. Having multiple people together either to learn something or to contribute their skills and authority can save a lot of time going back and forth independently. Remember to value your own time and the time of your participants when you create an agenda. If the value of the agenda does not justify the time participants—including you—will have to spend on it, don't call a meeting.

Resource for Success

Completing tasks requires the allocation of appropriate resources. It is important when distributing information about initiatives that are complex or that will require significant effort by one or more people, to consider all the resources that will be needed. People, information, time and priorities, technology, authority, and many other resources should be taken into consideration.

A common challenge that project managers experience is not having enough people to do the job. Make sure that the people resources allocated match the scope of the project. In addition, aligning the right people to the right tasks is critical. Having people with the appropriate skills is also important. If there is a skills gap, consider training or coaching your people, or perhaps hiring a consultant.

Projects can be stalled if there is a lack of information. Be sure to share as much information about the project as you can, both with project sponsors and project staff. In addition, it is very important to ensure that people working on the project team keep the purpose of the project top-of-mind. Knowing why tasks need to be completed is a strong motivator.

Time is often the resource that is not sufficiently considered before an initiative has been begun. A leader can create any number of stimulating initiatives, but if there isn't enough time for a person or team to implement them, you will end up with a bunch of half-finished initiatives that don't contribute much to the business. Make sure your people know how to prioritize the tasks that you give to them. Not every task can be top priority, and realistic prioritizing will help.

Be aware of what your people are already doing. Your reputation will suffer if your people think you don't know what projects are already consuming their time. That will lead to people feeling unimportant and will limit their desire to complete new tasks.

People need the physical tools to do their job. These will vary depending on your business and your objectives. In an office, this might include hardware, software, and workspace. In retail, it might be additional floor space, shelving, and inventory. Whatever your situation, be sure that people are not constrained because you have not taken the time to analyze their requirements and provide accordingly.

Ensure that your people have enough autonomy and authority to move their tasks forward. It is debilitating for them to have to repeatedly ask for permission to proceed. People need to know they are trusted. Giving them some level of authority over the completion of a task is a great way to show you trust them. Continue to inspect their work on a regular basis, but don't smother them with micro-management.

If a task needs to be completed, be sure the appropriate resources are available and allocated. We have described five of the most important resource types. Identifying and allocating the resources needed before a project is assigned will contribute significantly to a successful outcome.

Delegate, Don't Abdicate

Knowing how and when to delegate is crucial for any leader. Passing tasks to other people frees up your time to focus on other activities, like contemplating new growth or efficiency ideas. Delegating some of your tasks will allow for these important activities.

Assigning tasks to other people is also a benefit to them. It is very empowering for people to know that they are trusted, and that their contributions are valuable to the organization. There are so many different types of skills needed to run a successful business that a leader cannot possibly be the best at doing everything. If you are not delegating tasks, you will be missing out on utilizing some specialist skills that you personally don't possess. People with specialized skills need to be encouraged to soar. They will take the organization to new heights.

Delegating a task does not mean abdicating the responsibility for the task. If a task is worth doing, it is worth following up to ensure it has been completed, and that the desired outcome was achieved. But be reasonable with how often you follow-up; it is easy to follow up too often, and be perceived as interfering. One of the most common complaints in the workplace is that people feel micro-managed, as if they can't do anything without a manager constantly looking over their shoulder and correcting them. This type of management is crippling, and if left unchecked, will eventually suck the creative life out of the work force.

It is important for a leader to convey when a task must be done a certain way. This is different from wanting something done a certain way based on your own preference. Giving your people the autonomy to complete their tasks, sometimes in a way that isn't exactly how you would do it, can create an environment that stimulates productivity and creativity.

The key to good delegation is to make sure you have chosen the right people for the tasks. They need to have the skills and resources necessary. Be very clear about what is to be accomplished and by when. It is very empowering for people when at the outset, they know clearly what the parameters of the tasks are, and what constitutes a successful outcome. Let them know at what points, and at what intervals, you expect progress reports.

Never assume that you don't need to follow up because the person to whom you have delegated a task is a great worker. Don't abdicate this crucial step. Following up keeps you in the loop, underscores the importance of the task, and shows the person to whom you have delegated the task that you care. From a practical perspective, you want to know if everything is going to plan, and if there is anything you can do to help.

Leadership is about giving clear objectives, delegating to the right people, and then supporting them in what they do. Give them the tools and the guidance, and then stand back and let them perform. Measure performance and give feedback, so that people know when they hit a target and what they need to do if they missed it.

People happily take on tasks when they know they will be given the chance to complete them without continual harassment. Micro-management is a poor leadership style. Treating people like puppets, pulling their strings whenever you feel the need to show who is in control will only stifle productivity.

Work on Two Sides of the Business

To lead a sustainable business you need to work on two sides of the business. One side is about the product or service you supply to your customers. The other side is the administration of the business. In other words; taking care of your customers and taking care of your business.

It isn't quite as cut and dried as that, of course, because many aspects of your business can be classified in both categories. Generally speaking, it is important to recognize that there are two sides to a business, and both require ongoing attention.

(There is a third side to the business that also requires attention. The third side could be called "developing your business", and we will discuss this aspect in the next chapter.)

Continuous focus on the customer experience is vital to ensure you maintain a positive presence in the market. If for any reason, customers find your service unacceptable, regardless of how well you take care of your business, the outlook isn't good. Equally, if you don't take care of your business, even if your customers shower your product or service with praise, the outlook is poor.

To illustrate the two sides of a business, let's consider a car as if it were a business. The service a car provides is to take the driver from A to B. Some of the beneficial, customer-facing features include the speed it is capable of, the comfort of the drive, the entertainment system, the number of passengers it can accommodate, and so on. Taking care of the business includes; filling the gas tank, keeping the tires pumped up, doing regular maintenance, being careful of how you drive, and where you park it. The price of the car is a good example of concerns that could fall in both categories. The car must be priced to attract a customer—taking care of the customer—and priced to create a positive profit margin for the business—taking care of the business.

The following story shows how neglecting one side of the business can cause a serious problem. A retail outlet on a busy street was always full of customers. Their products were clearly in high demand, their customer service was pleasing, and their pricing seemed reasonable. It seemed like they had the right recipe for long term success. One day, without any notice, the shop was shuttered. There was a notice pinned to the door explaining that the business was no longer in operation, and apologizing to all of the customers who had been loyal to the shop over the years.

The business had clearly experienced some severe difficulties. Their top-selling products were providing very thin margins, and so the economics had always been tight. As a result, the business was unable to pay competitive wages, and maintaining long term staff had been difficult. The owner frequently had to work long hours in the shop, and this affected his health. Because the accounting was not being handled by a professional, when a large unexpected debt came due, it could not be covered.

This is a sad case study, but one that serves to illustrate how crucial it is to work on both sides of the business.

Paying close attention to your customers' experience is crucial. But don't neglect the administration of your business. You owe it to yourself and to your employees to pay close attention to how your business is running in order to maintain a healthy and sustainable condition—if you cannot stay in business, then the world will lose the service that your company can provide.

Stay Focused

Staying focused is a key ability for leadership. If you are easily distracted and find it hard to complete things, your people will lose the desire to follow you. A common denominator we have noticed in the biographies of historic leaders is a single-minded focus to achieve their objectives. You may not always have

"Nothing of value is realized if nothing of value is completed."

all the information you require in your initial plan, but by being focused and determined, and giving clear instructions for implementation, you give your plan a better chance to succeed.

Staying focused requires having clear objectives and following them through to completion. To stay focused on an objective, or a set of objectives, you have to define them first. You need a broad overall objective for your company, which will be used to set departmental and specific job objectives. Beyond that, you should always be setting further objectives that refine processes and improve the productivity in your area of responsibility. Ensure you are not just making work for people. Your objectives should be measurable and beneficial to the business. This will enhance the buy-in needed from those who are tasked with the implementation. Following through on a project, either to a desired outcome or until the project is halted, is important for creating credibility in the future.

Providing feedback to people about the conclusion and outcome of the objective will close the loop, and give you the opportunity to appreciate the efforts of those involved.

After you have identified an objective, and before you have given directions for the implementation, ensure that everyone who is involved or affected by the objective knows what to expect. Having to deal with side issues that arise from your objectives can take you off course and seriously disrupt your focus. Before you know it, you can be working on a resolution to a problem that takes you in a completely different direction.

Be aware of how your work can affect other departments who may not be aware of what you are doing. Unexpected or unintended effects from your projects can create waves of disturbance for others, and can cause frustration and distraction. While it is good to have a reputation for being innovative, be careful that you don't take your people off course with too many new ideas. This will only serve to confuse what the priorities should be. Having too many projects will dilute their attention, and yours.

Staying focused requires knowing what milestones need to be achieved and keeping track of the current stage of your project. To truly achieve your desired outcome, consider this William Edwards Deming quote: "You can expect what you inspect." Leaving a project to other people quickly sends the message that you attach little or no importance to it. Keep in touch with those responsible for completing tasks and, if necessary, play an active role to ensure that actions are completed.

Focus is about seeing something through to its conclusion. After the objective has been reached, be sure to make some kind of note for yourself. This will reinforce your ability to stay focused and get things done. Many of us have been conditioned to think that we never complete anything; consciously noting when we complete a task will help with our reprogramming. Also, be sure to compliment those who have been involved in achieving the objective; this will give them a sense of completion.

Always strive to have worthy objectives, and identify everyone who will be involved or affected by your plans. Clearly define the purpose and implementation plans for your objective, and then employ a single-minded focus until your objective has been achieved.

Know When to Change Course

Knowing your business well enough to identify change signals will give you a valuable edge in the market. Being able to adjust your course to avoid a pitfall or to take advantage of a window of opportunity can make a material difference in your productivity. Often, the effectiveness of a leader can be judged by the ability to minimize the down-swings and maximize the good times. To be effective, you need to have a good understanding of all the metrics in your business and be very aware of the market conditions.

Consider seasonal changes and how they impact your business. For example, the buying patterns in the summer may be significantly different from those in the winter. A government year-end might create a flurry of activity for you. Seasonal changes are easy to predict and plan for, but what if something unexpected happens: are you prepared?

A worse problem may be a small change in business productivity that you haven't noticed. Over time, a small change can eat away at your business until it becomes a big problem that could take significant action to address.

Constantly probing your business, even in areas that seem to be functioning well, will ensure that you see the early signs that changes are happening. The evolution of your business might be obvious when defined by key milestones over the years, but the very small items that create the momentum are often overlooked.

So if the data entry backlog looks fine, why bother analyzing it? If the days outstanding for account receivables look consistent, why bother discussing it? If the service and price from Supplier X is fine, why bother getting comparative quotes? These kinds of questions can be asked in hundreds or even thousands of small seemingly inconsequential areas of your business. The fact is this; if you are not paying attention to these kinds of business metrics, you probably don't know your business well enough, and that will cost you, maybe not today, but certainly at some point.

Be sure to follow all of the underlying metrics of your business. This will ensure that there are no nasty surprises waiting just around the corner. Sometimes change occurs, and we don't notice until it's either too late, or drastic action is needed. If this happens, ensure that your people know who takes responsibility for what in an emergency and be clear about what authority levels they have. Often a change in circumstances, even disastrous ones, can uncover new learning opportunities that make the business even stronger.

Refine Processes

Always be on the lookout for ways to refine your business processes. There is nothing more ridiculous than someone responding to the question, "Why do you do it this way?" with, "Because it has always been done this way". One of the biggest time wasters in your business is people doing things that they don't have to do.

Worse than a waste of time, is discovering that a process is actually working against company objectives. For example, suppose the shipping department process required packing an extra unit in case one of the units was damaged in transit. Since the time that process was created, a product upgrade made it more durable. Because no one evaluated the process and renewed it, your company is literally shipping your profits out of the door.

Processes that produce a good outcome are often not reviewed. Ignoring them is a mistake because these processes camouflage unnecessary costs. If you do something a certain way because it gets the job done, and nobody complains because they think it is not an important part of the business, the process is ignored.

The key error is the thought that it is not an important part of the business. If you are fulfilling a process that is not important to the business, why are you doing it? It is likely that it is important, but it has been deemed too unimportant to be inspected. If this is an attitude that has infected your business, you must stamp it out.

Reviewing your business processes is like painting the Sydney Harbour Bridge—it takes so long to complete, that by the time the painting has reached the end of the bridge, it's time to start painting at the other end again. Reviewing and updating your processes is a never-ending task. Delegation of responsibility for this task to your department managers is necessary, but as a business leader, you should take responsibility for following up.

If you haven't been diligent in this area, you might find some glaring, "low hanging fruit" problems that you can solve quickly, saving time and money, and improving productivity immediately. Refining your processes regularly will keep your business efficient, fresh, and up-to-date with current objectives.

LEADING BUSINESS SUMMARY

Spending time taking care of the running of your business is key to your success. Business knowledge enables you to add value to the business beyond your expected performance.

The table below highlights the abilities discussed in this section, followed by the positive behaviours that characterize them. The Negative Behaviour column highlights behaviours you will notice if these abilities have not been developed.

Abilities	Positive Behaviours	Negative Behaviours
Knows the business in data terms	Knows all areas of business; decisions are knowledge-based	Limited business knowledge
Is informed	Gathers information from many different people	Unaware of day-to-day happenings
Sees the complete picture	Congruent with company objectives	Acts contrary to company direction
Is organized	Has clear priorities: prepared, calm	Flustered, overwhelmed
Leads from the front and from the rear	Leads by handing off the baton when appropriate	Must be in control at all times
Applies a decision making process	Makes sound, consistent decisions	Inconsistent; procrastinates
Has productive meetings	Meetings are well-run; things get accomplished	Meetings are a waste of time
Resources for success	People know what and how, and have the tools to do their tasks	Everyone is overworked and frustrated

Abilities	Positive Behaviours	Negative Behaviours
Delegates but does not abdicate	Delegates responsibility and is kept informed	Micro-manages
Works on two sides of the business	Spends time in the back office, and on the customer	Business survival in jeopardy
Stays focused	Everyone always knows what to do	No one knows what priorities are
Knows when to change course	Watches for signals to change	Caught unaware
Refines processes	Always looking to improve the business; pays attention to detail	Processes become bloated and inefficient

Executive

INTRODUCTION

Getting to the Executive level is a major achievement. At this level, you have the responsibility for the economic well-being of many people. While you probably have people you can share your thoughts with, and who will give you feedback, you will often be responsible for making final decisions.

You must be aware of, and follow, changing business compliance guidelines. You must remain centred on your principles, and on the mission of your business, while trying to develop the business under ever-changing conditions. You are expected to be self-directed, and it is common for an executive to be the senior person in a location.

As the eyes and ears for the Board of Directors or the shareholders, it is important for an executive to know what is going on in the company, yesterday and today, and what is expected tomorrow. As important as it is to share information up the line, it is equally important to be able to share information down the line. People expect executives to have their fingers on the pulse, and if an executive gives evidence of being out of touch, it will reverberate throughout the company.

Key executives will often set the culture for the entire company. People judge executives by the decisions they make. One of the primary decisions involves the guidelines set for the working environment. This and many other management decisions will create the perceptions that people have of an executive, and once these perceptions are set, they are very difficult to change. Unfavourable perceptions can have a significant impact on how well the business develops.

It is difficult to implement strategies in a complex organization. If the people are reluctant or too compliant, the business growth will be hampered.

It makes sense that, as you climb the ladder of corporate success, the pressure and demands increase. Being an executive is not a good fit for everyone, but for those who do find it a good fit, it can be very stimulating. While the pressures are greater, so are the rewards. If you find pleasure in directing business, or developing people, or earning a high income, or seeing your goals come to fruition, there are plenty of rewards to choose from.

Just because you have made it to the corner office, though, it doesn't mean the learning stops. In this chapter we will discuss the abilities that you must develop to ensure that you are seen as a good executive, and to keep your business moving forward. Developing these abilities will enable you to keep your foot on your career accelerator.

Be the Commander

People who command properly generate respect that motivates others to willingly go the distance. People who command poorly resort to intimidation. Working with an intimidator generally produces compliance but little else. Commanding requires the abilities—highly developed—that we are describing throughout this book.

You are reaching the pinnacle of your abilities, and starting to understand that your value is measured by how well you serve others. A person who knows how to command has confidence that is not ego-based. Commanders have charisma, an energy that attracts people to them. Others do not need to know the commander's name or position; they just sense the energy and want to be near it.

Commanders do not consider themselves to be better than other people; in fact, commanders don't even think in those terms. Everyone plays a pivotal role in the delivery of a product or service, and commanders understand this. By contrast, intimidators see people as disposable commodities necessary to fulfil a task.

A commander creates a vivid image of where the business is going, how it can make a difference, and what part each person will play in the process. This kind of leadership creates an environment that people want to be a part of. People don't work just for the money, in fact when one earns enough to meet basic needs, money slips quickly down the priority list; people want to be a part of something that counts. A commander helps them fulfil this need.

Are you considered a commander? Ask yourself these questions:

◊　If your business requires painful commitment to overcome a challenge, will your people willingly follow you?

◊　Do they trust you to represent their business, and to safeguard their future?

◊　Do the people care about the service they provide, and talk proudly about it whenever the opportunity arises?

◊　Have you cultivated an environment that encourages people to grow beyond their current level of responsibility?

If you can answer "Yes" to all of these questions, you may be ready to take the next step: the step to the Visionary level.

Although it isn't an easy path, anyone can get to the executive level. Following the right process to develop your capabilities will ultimately put you there.

Be Strategic

The development of strategic objectives occurs at the highest level of executive responsibility. Everything else flows from the strategy. It provides the direction senior managers use to create the plans to achieve the strategic objectives. The plans flow to the managers whose job it is to ensure that the people know what to do, and how to do it.

Strategy is largely influenced by the executives currently in office. The emphasis on "currently" is important, because different people will have different views on how a business should be developed, and their influence can be significant. Taking into account many variables such as the business sector, the economy, the history of the business, and the current financial status, the executives will decide on the short and long term objectives.

Also important to the success of any strategy is the communication of the strategic objectives to the employees. In the Leadership chapter, we discussed two sides of the business; taking care of the customer and taking care of business administration. At the Executive level, the third side of the pyramid is defined; taking care of business development.

There are two fundamental questions the executive team will ask when creating a strategic plan. "How can we grow the business (or stop the decline)" and, "What are our plans for the business?" The answers to these very broad questions should be refined until a clear prescription for action can be developed.

Suppose the answer to the first question involves creating massive growth. While that objective might sound like one that every company should set, it really depends on the conditions inside and outside the business. Creating massive growth requires commitment of investment. The culture of a business in massive growth mode is very different from that of a company involved in steady organic growth. If a company commits to a massive growth objective, it needs to have the resources to do so; otherwise the result could be very damaging. Of course, the market has to play ball, too. If your sector isn't ready to support high growth, you may be wasting your money chasing an unobtainable goal.

The answer to the second question is also critical: "What are your plans for the business?" Imagine that there is a desire to sell the business in the near term, or perhaps merge with another business, or develop products for new markets. If your business is small but developing fast, maybe your goal is to take the business public, which could create wealth for the founders while raising cash for the business to invest in future growth.

Taking a company public can be both exhilarating and very challenging. Working in a publicly traded company requires following significant compliance procedures, and sharing information that was previously held close to the owner's vest. It affects many people throughout the organization, and is not a decision that should be taken lightly, or with dollar signs in the owner's eyes. Whether public or private, the strategic plans for the business have a significant influence on how the business is run.

Communicating strategy to all the employees of the business is important. It is confusing for the employees to be given tasks that do not seem to be in concert with the generally known mission of the company, or if it is discovered that a major event occurred that nobody knew about in advance. Not all strategic objectives can be shared with employees, particularly if the business is publicly traded. However, hiding behind the rules of governance to keep workers in the dark is unlikely to serve your business well.

Being honest and open with employees will always increase the respect and the loyalty of your team; even if it means telling them that some information cannot be widely shared until later in their implementation. People understand that there are compliance rules to be followed to ensure fair business practice, and that competitive secrets can't be shared ahead of time.

Creating a strategic plan for a company is vitally important. Companies that don't have a clear strategic plan will find they are lacking in leadership—never a good position to be in. Your strategic plan will set the direction that will ultimately affect every person employed in the business. It will also define the short and medium term objectives for the business. Being clear about the capabilities of the business, having knowledge of the market place, and being realistic with objectives should all provide useful guidance about what your strategy should look like. Ensure that employees are as well informed of the strategy as they can be. Finally, infuse your strategic plans with sincerity and a genuine desire to serve your community.

Most important: remember that you are at a level of responsibility that goes far beyond your own ego.

Inspire

Inspiring people is about how you communicate a common cause for people to achieve with you. If you are able to deliver a message that inspires your people to drive your initiatives to completion, you will be able to achieve the full potential of your organization.

To be successful, the cause must be congruent with the mission of the organization. This will ensure that the message does not lead to confusion and mismanagement. Many different groups of people must be inspired independently.

If you are several levels higher in the organization than the people who execute the tasks, you need to ensure that your senior management team has a clear understanding of what your directives are. If they do not know what you want, there is a good chance that, by the time the directions have been received by the workers, they will be significantly different from your original intent.

To be inspired, people need to know who is calling the shots, and what they are expected to do to be successful. In the more traditional organizational hierarchy, executives who don't work in the same location as the workers need to be seen, and they need to demonstrate that they know what it takes to complete a task. They need to consistently show that they are not isolated in an ivory tower, making decisions that do not consider the impact on people's lives.

Over the past few decades, a flatter, less hierarchical, organization chart has become more common. While this enables the executives to be seen and known by the workers, executives need to be careful that they do not lose the authority that is a necessary part of their responsibility. People need to be able to clearly identify who the leaders are.

Take the time to connect with people at all levels. Not only will this be motivating to the staff, it will also serve to give you a good understanding of how the business is being run, where it really counts.

If you are able to keep refining your products and show a genuine interest in your customers, you are laying the foundation on which to regularly inspire your people to perform at a world-class level.

Inspired people will talk to their friends about the company they work for. People want to be proud of their company, to be able to talk about the services they provide, and their great working conditions. What your people think and say about the company is an important barometer of your success.

Be proud of your business, and when there are problems, don't pretend they don't exist or that they don't matter; they do matter, and they should be addressed.

To inspire your team, keep the mission of the business central in your mind. Make sure your senior management team has a clear understanding of what you want to achieve. Regularly review and understand the conditions under which your people are working. Remind your customers who you are and how you provide your service. With these items under control, your decisions and messaging should flow intuitively.

Inspiring your workforce should not be saved for a special occasion. Look for opportunities to sincerely inspire your people, and in return, they will take care of your business.

Show Respect

Respecting other people and their values is very powerful, particularly for those at a senior level. It is a sad fact that people generally go through life seeking approval from others, in one form or another. As a senior person in your organization, your approval will carry a lot of importance with your staff.

Respect can take many forms: respect for an alternative opinion, respect for cultural differences, and the career development and personal needs of those around you. An ounce of respect in any of these areas can inspire a person to loyalty for their entire career.

The ability to accept the differing views of other people is required to move up in levels of authority. Respecting others, and showing it, is required long before you reach the Executive level, but at this level of responsibility, it becomes even more important and in some ways, a tougher test. At the Executive level, you have responsibility for people who are leaders in their own right. To stifle their opinions is not only disrespectful; it also limits the contribution they can bring to the organization. At the Executive level, you have to be even more conscious of allowing opinions that differ from your own.

Allowing other opinions, though, does not mean accepting input that you do not think is valid. But being open to opinion and including it in your own contemplation will add insight that you may not have considered. If you do not agree with the opinion of one of your senior team, take the time to discuss why. This will show your senior team members that you are a reasonable person. Even when you do not eventually act on their input, you are willing to share your thoughts. When you do accept their opinion, it will validate your desire to provide not just your solution, but the best solution.

Respecting cultural differences is not optional, if you wish to have any success at all working with a person or business in which there is cultural diversity. Experiencing new cultures can be exhilarating, and will broaden your knowledge of the world. However, respecting a culture does not mean you have to study and be fully conversant with it. Knowing something about a different culture will surely help, but it is not required. If you are not judgemental, and you are willing to accept differences, that is a good place to start. If you have the good fortune to work in different countries, make it a point to learn more about the culture either by reading, or by asking questions, and by paying attention to the cultural differences around you. If you work with people who have personal cultures different from your own, including religious or lifestyle choices, remember that you are as different to them as they are to you.

If a culture is offensive to you, ask yourself why. It usually stems from an issue that you have been conditioned to in the past, and your HMw is giving you conflicting signals. Ultimately, whatever the differences in culture might be, we all need to work together. Respecting other cultures will not only make your working environment more productive, it will also serve as a growth experience for you.

Respecting people means that, as leader, you have the responsibility to help others develop their careers and move from one level of responsibility to another. If you are so wrapped up in quarterly statements and press releases, it is easy to lose sight of the value your people represent and the need they have for your attention. Almost every annual report ever printed includes a statement about the value of their people. When we read remarkably similar statements so often, it makes us wonder if the statement truly reflects reality, or if it's just boilerplate copy to be inserted every year.

Respect the need for your people to grow. To prove you mean it, take a personal interest, and invest the time for involvement. The more time and energy you invest in sincerely getting to know your people and helping them to grow, the more they will invest in helping your business grow.

Respect the importance of work and home-life balance. As you get deeply involved in important matters that require working at unsociable hours, or you have travel time away from home, you place a stress upon those who rely on you. It may be that your life mission is all consuming and you want to devote all your waking hours to it. While this can be inspiring, don't discard those with whom you have chosen to share your life. Their mission is also important. Respect the work and home-life balance of your employees, too.

Before making judgements about a person's work commitment, consider the following common situations that may be affecting those you work with; raising children, being a single parent, having a sick or infirm dependant, taking care of elderly parents, or being involved in a community project. It is amazing how your previous judgement of someone's personal needs will change once you experience a similar situation yourself. Don't fall into the trap of assuming someone is not committed just because they duck out of a meeting. Everyone has personal conditions to consider; being respectful of this fact will create valuable loyalty.

The word "respect" carries a lot of power. Your approval is very important to your staff. You can't just claim to be respectful and expect people to accept your word. You need to understand a person or group in order to sincerely respect their contributions and their differences. Respect is a strong motivator that encourages people to do their best.

Stay Competitive

Being competitive is a powerful executive characteristic. Some define "competitive" in the Machiavellian sense of winning at all costs, or in the sports sense of striving to be the winner rather than the loser. Here, we define "competitive" as a burning desire to complete your objectives. Your objectives may include: serving your customers in the very best way you can, and as often as you can; building your business into a sustainable and important part of the market place; creating a working environment that keeps and attracts people who want to grow; and helping your people move from one level of responsibility to another. Your burning competitive desire to achieve your objectives is as real and as energetic as that of the fighter stepping into the ring to face an opponent. Your focus is not on dropping an opponent to the mat, but rather on providing a world-class service.

You need to know what your marketplace looks like. What other companies are working in the same space? What do they do that you could do better? What do you do that gives you a unique selling proposition? The free market environment is a critical component to the achievement of all our hopes and dreams; it is a major cause that people fight to preserve. Ultimately, the free market ensures that the very best service at the very best pricing is made available to the consumer. A free market will result in the attrition of some companies.

You would not be serving your customers, suppliers and employees well if you ignored the competition in your market place. But your service is not designed to destroy other companies. If the only way you can succeed is by destroying the competition and if that cause is central to your strategy, you will probably lose, if not now, then at some point in the future. Instead, focusing on the positive aspects of what your business can provide will give you a chance to rise above the crowd.

A competitive attitude to the internal development of your organization is important too. Striving to be bigger, better, stronger, and faster by developing great products, refining your processes, and training your people well will create a dynamic environment as competitive as any sporting event. The people in your business need to be aware of, and challenged by, its objectives. Accomplishments are measured in a variety of ways, and having a competitive environment is very conducive to good productivity.

Winning means to successfully provide the very best service to as many people as you can, and as often as you can. It means building a business that is sustainable and provides the opportunity for people to provide their services as part of the common goal.

Losing is not an option. This means that it is unthinkable for there to be a world in which your services are not delivered. You will focus all of your power to ensure that your company does whatever it can to be the leader in its market place. This will mean that some companies will come and go, but your energy is not wasted worrying about other companies; your energy is channelled exclusively on how your business can become bigger, better, stronger, and faster.

You are highly competitive in the positive sense and your principles are a driving factor that attracts workers, suppliers, and customers.

Respond to Challenges

When major challenges are presented to your business, how do you respond? As we have mentioned before, the evolution of a business is defined by the way it responds to challenges. The organization's response is generally influenced by the mindset of the executives who make the decisions. Challenges are often viewed as problems, but in the same way that a person can learn from every situation and evolve, so can a business. As we learned when we talked about the responsibilities of being a leader, don't assume that as an executive, you have all the answers. After the challenge has been defined and a desired outcome has been agreed on, make sure that the right people are assigned to create the response plan. They might be members of the executive team, but often you will include members of the management team, too. Being creative is important, and so is being practical and realistic.

David was involved in a major strategic initiative that was required in the wake of a global economic decline. The executive team defined the problems, agreed on the desired outcome, and then a team made up of executives and senior managers created a plan. David and a fellow executive who had both been intimately involved in the development of the plan were tasked with its implementation. The mission ahead was clear; project the declining revenue to the lowest point, ensure the business would stay profitable at that level and create the conditions for future growth.

Everything was to be assessed including number of employees, marketing costs, supplier services, products available to the market, and much more. When a business experiences a severe revenue decline, the response is not just about closing the wound; the response also has to ensure the business is strong enough afterwards to return to a sustainable condition. During the planning and implementation of the response, creativity had to be applied to all existing activities to enable continuation. For example, a detailed reporting process had to be established to define how many sales people should be retained. Too few would make it difficult to serve the existing demand for the products and limit the turn-around capabilities. Too many would be costly and create an environment in which the sales people would not be able to reach their desired compensation targets.

During this situation, the business leaders developed new geographic revenue streams that contributed significantly to stabilizing the business. A new form of product delivery was initiated in the darkest hours that would later provide a significant source of revenue, and could one day serve as the catalyst for an entirely new business model. One of the most important things that contributed to the success of this mission was communication. Coordinated through the Human Resources group, people were continually provided with updates. Actions affecting staff were coordinated to happen simultaneously, to reduce the impact of the rumour mill, and to allow employee fears to be addressed openly and collectively.

In a crisis situation, we learn a lot about our business, the character of the leaders, and our ability to respond under pressure. It is never a pleasant experience to have to make decisions that affect people's lives in a negative way, but when these decisions are presented to you, be sure you are equal to the challenge. Be creative, include the skills of others, and remain committed to providing your best services to the many people who rely on you for guidance.

Position Your Business

Positioning your business to remain current with the provision of your services to the market will exercise your visionary abilities. Most fundamental changes in an industry take several years to become the new standards. Even revolutionary changes that, in hindsight, appear to have happened very quickly, usually take a year or two to complete. Being able to predict changes will put you in a position to have a small window of opportunity to enjoy significant growth before the other companies in your sector catch up.

It is possible that your core services or products are in a market that does not change, but that is rare. Today, the window of opportunity for a business to provide its service without revision is very small. At some point, your product or your branding will have to be revised to appeal to a changing audience. The way you market your product may need to change, or you may have to change the way you deliver your product. Whatever the situation, it is important that you pay conscious attention to the positioning of your business, so that you can change course before you hit the rocks.

The software industry is a good example of the need for companies to continually revise products, and reposition themselves. Technology has influenced a continual change in many of the daily products we use. Every year, the latest version of a product becomes the centre point of the company's revenue production. Being late to the market, or providing inefficient or insufficient features, can destroy a brand and send a multi-national business into a tailspin.

Having a finger on the pulse of your sector is critical in recognizing the signs of future market swings. If you are able to create changes in your sector, this will clearly give you an important edge on the competitive landscape.

Most companies have seen a paradigm shift over the last decade or so, in the way they market their products. The advent of the internet and online marketing has significantly changed how a company reaches out to its prospective customers. Those companies who stick to their old ways are either going out of business, struggling, or possibly, they have a very solid niche market that does not require an online presence. The speed and stability of online delivery also facilitated a change to the way some organizations deliver their product.

> *"A player out of position will rarely receive the ball."*

Positioning of your business is vital for its sustainability. Whether it is what you provide, how you provide it, or how you market it, you and your business must have a mature process for continually evaluating your position. Investing in market research, keeping close contact with your product development people and most importantly, staying in close contact with your customers, will help you to ensure that you maintain a productive and successful position.

Demonstrate Geographical Cultural Awareness

The cultural differences between cities and countries require that a business pay particular attention to how they market and deliver their services, and also the working environment for their employees. Assuming that a model that works in a big city in North America will also work in Europe or in the Far East is a mistake. Likewise, expecting that a model that is successful in one European country will also fit all of the other countries is also a mistake.

David has led businesses in countries around the world and he has learned that cultural differences can be the number one challenge for an international business model. For example, the US is typically oriented toward quarterly results, continuous focus is placed on head count, and customer price incentives are commonplace.

The United Kingdom, while also profit-driven, is not as driven by quarterly results. The employment rules in the UK are more favourable to the employee than they are in the US, and customer promotions are not everyday occurrences.

Some European countries are very employee-centric, and making strategic decisions has to include what is and is not acceptable to employees.

In the Far East, cultures are so different from those in Europe and North America that it is advisable to employ an expert in the local culture to ensure that you don't seriously offend people, or break local laws.

If executives of a business do not travel to the countries in which they operate, the local business often feels that they are poorly represented. Local culture can then take on a different and more locally meaningful purpose, which might even stretch to support local positions that are contrary to that of the company head office. International offices can easily become independent of the corporate head office if left alone too long.

In offices remote from head office, there is already a feeling of international independence just because of the distance. If the executives do not take the time necessary to stay connected, new systems, processes, and even new products will surface in the remote office, and it can become very messy to realign the remote office to the corporate objectives. This is compounded if the international/remote business is doing well. It's easy to ignore what seems to be working. After it stops working, and you need to find out why—that's when the hard work really starts.

It is often stated that we all live and work in a global community. This may be true when it comes to communicating and conducting business on an international basis. Do not, however, assume that a global community means we all live and work by the same rules. Don't become complacent. Check in with your own international businesses frequently, and be sure to stay open to the differences, even when they don't sound rational to you.

Culture is very important to us all and being respectful of cultural differences will help you to understand and work with the differences.

Build Credibility

Credibility can be defined as the impression that leads others to accept your opinions and conclusions. When you have credibility, people will accept what you say because they see you as a reliable source. This is very important for implementing strategies and major decisions. A work force that does not believe that their executives are credible may do what they are told, but not much more than that. In some cases, particularly where work locations are geographically dispersed, decisions can be ignored or reworked to fit the thoughts of those in the distant locations.

Whether people accept you as credible depends on what they think of you, and how consistent you are.

How will people form an opinion of you? People will gauge your credibility based on your experience relating to the role that you fulfil and your understanding of the everyday routines of your business. People also gauge your credibility based on how you conduct yourself in their presence, and in public. The degree to which people feel they know you and your value to the business will either increase or decrease your credibility in their minds.

It is vitally important in building credibility with your work force that you pay close attention at a detailed level to how your business is run. You need to be fully conversant with the processes your business employs and, as much as possible, get to know the people who play key roles. This, at a minimum, should be the early objective of any incoming executive. If an executive does not pay attention to the workings of their current business and does not get to know the people they work with, the road ahead is likely to be very bumpy, and probably quite short.

The most effective way for people to get to know you is for you to get to know them. People like to know that senior leaders understand and respect their work. Asking people what they do, how they do it, and what particular skills are required to perform their tasks will give you good insight into their contribution. Asking these types of questions will not only raise your credibility in the minds of your people, but will also provide you with valuable information for the running of the business.

Often, people who have not yet experienced the executive level wonder what an executive does. They don't actually see you do anything in the business, so what do you do? The answer is simple. Understanding at a deep level what is occurring in the business, in all areas of the business, takes a significant amount of time. It is vital to the safe progress of the business that all executives devote enough time to gaining this understanding.

The second aspect affecting your credibility is the consistency of your actions. If your actions continually swing from one direction to another, people will become confused and you will lose credibility. For example, setting up a project team to develop a product, dismantling it without apparent cause, and then restarting it again will leave people confused. When there is poor consistency, people will feel stressed, and the credibility of the executives leading the business will be called into doubt. Business needs do change, sometimes frequently. All it takes to help people to understand the context of your decisions is ongoing communication about the current strategic direction of the company, and how current actions feed into that direction.

Throughout your career, you have made many decisions, and you have probably become very confident in doing so. This is a very good ability to have developed. But you must be careful not to become complacent, or ignore the need that people have to understand what is going on. An executive has the power to make decisions that affect hundreds or thousands of people. Those people deserve to know what the broad objectives are, and why particular decisions are being made.

When people have a sense of who you are, they can relate to you on a personal level. They can then associate the decisions with the person making them. The alternative is that people think decisions are being made by some unknown executive who can't possibly know what it really takes to do the work. If people understand the company objectives and see consistency in your actions, you will enjoy the benefits of being credible. Your decisions will be accepted easily, and the business will run more smoothly.

EXECUTIVE SUMMARY

At the Executive level, you have the responsibility for the economic well-being of many people. Although you have people with whom to share your thoughts and gain feedback, you make the final decisions. You need to stay true to your principles and the mission of your business, while trying to develop the business under variable conditions.

Here is the summary table outlining the Executive level abilities and the key positive behaviours associated with each ability. The Negative Behaviours listed in the last column describe the behaviours exhibited when the Executive abilities have not been developed.

Abilities	Positive Behaviours	Negative Behaviours
Commanding	Is respected; people follow because they know it will benefit them	People do what they are told and no more
Strategic	Knows where company is headed and how to get there	People do their own thing and there is no real direction from the top
Inspiring	Creates and communicates worthy goals	Lives in ivory tower; people don't know them
Respectful	Respects others' opinions and differences	Bulldozer; fixed opinions
Competitive	Has burning desire to complete objectives	Ambivalent; loses focus
Responds to challenges	Creative, practical, and realistic responses to challenges	Relies on chance
Positions business	Changes face of business to meet market demands	Does not move with the times
Demonstrates geographical and cultural awareness	Pays attention to local cultures, applies culturally appropriate models	Forces own customs when doing business in foreign countries
Builds credibility	Behaves with integrity and consistency; gets to know the people	Inconsistent and distant; people don't know them

Design

At the Design stage, you are at the very pinnacle of human production. What you do now will define the landscape that many will work on.

This stage contains the final step of the Career Acceleration Process.

Step 7: Visionary—Defining and implementing your vision

Visionary

INTRODUCTION

As a Visionary, you have passed through the stages defined as Me, Us, and Them and now you are at the stage that is defined as Everyone. It is at this level that your service can influence the broader community.

Through your career, you have continuously developed your abilities, and in doing so, you have travelled through the levels of responsibility. Your progressive development process has brought you to the top step, Visionary. There is one almost visible difference between a visionary and everyone else: they love what they do. Visionaries don't "work" in the everyday sense of the word; they are in a relationship with their cause. It takes more effort to stop what they do than to start. Even when they aren't actively involved in tasks to develop their vision, they are thinking about it.

It's like having your first boyfriend or girlfriend. You just can't stop thinking about them, and you are happiest when you are spending time with them. Could there be a better job than this?

You enjoy teaching people at this level; but not in the form of an intermediary of information who transfers knowledge from a book or another person. At this level, the source of knowledge is you. You teach from your own experiences, and your analysis of those experiences, and your knowledge is unique. You seek opportunities to teach other, both one-on-one, and through your actions, and through the products and services you design. Your contribution will take people in a new direction of thought and will inspire people to consider new ways of approaching familiar situations.

Defining a Visionary

We are all capable of having visions. We see a new way that a commonly-used product or service could work better than it does now. Through many years of experience, we develop a unique perspective on a particular area of public service. We might even get a flash of inspiration and a totally new concept forms in our mind. This last example happens frequently and you may even have experienced it yourself. You may have had a flash of inspiration about a particular product or service and then, one day, there it was, in common use. You might have thought, "Hey that was my idea!"

We have discussed setting personal career goals and planning for their realization, and this process is quite similar to what is required to realize your vision. Unlike a personal goal, however, your vision is not just about you. It will affect a broader community, and so the implementation requires additional abilities. There will usually be more obstacles on your path and many more aspects of the projects that are not in your control. Having a vision is easy; implementing it is much more challenging. It is the successful implementation of your vision that defines you as a visionary.

There have been many great Visionaries throughout history whose contributions have influenced millions of people. To name just a few; John Hancock, Samuel Adams, Mahatma Ghandi, Nelson Mandela, Thomas Edison, Bill Gates, Steve Jobs; and the list goes on. These visionaries influenced and improved the lives of others on a massive scale. When you read the names of people who have achieved great things, you may be inspired and imagine what it might be like to be one of these people. But then, the tendency is to fall back into reality and let your visions evaporate, because you convince yourself that you are not as good as they are.

The truth is: you are like these people. You can be great. So the question should be, "What is the difference between them and me?" And here is the secret. These people get their visions from the same sources that you do; it is what they do with their vision that makes them exceptional. They turn their visions into reality.

A worthy vision isn't defined by its scope of impact or how widely known it becomes. While it's wonderful to aspire to the levels of service that influence all of humanity, and we all have it within us to realize visions of this magnitude if that is our calling, being a visionary doesn't mean your vision has to be realized on a global basis. Your vision may have an impact on a local community, a town, a city, a country, or it might influence people globally. Having a smaller scope or size does not diminish the vision.

The following sections describe the abilities you will require to implement your vision.

Be Receptive to Inspiration

An important ability that visionaries have is that they use their imaginations, and allow themselves to be inspired. Albert Einstein found that his most important discoveries came, not when he was thinking, but when he allowed his imagination to roam. Said Einstein, "Imagination is more important than knowledge, for knowledge is limited to all we now know and understand, while imagination embraces the entire world, and all there ever will be to know and understand." We all have these imagination moments, when ideas seem to pop out of thin air and into our heads.

Whether we call it inspiration, imagination, or intuition, and whether we say that it comes from somewhere deep within, or from connecting with something beyond ourselves, visionaries are able to let go, and let creativity in. They plug into an energy that they may call inner wisdom, nature, the universe, or even God, and allow this energy source to inspire and even help manifest their visions.

If you allow yourself to, you can plug in, too. If you are able to stay focused on an objective for any length of time, you will receive thoughts and ideas, whether from within or beyond, that contribute to your objective. The thoughts you will receive won't be just "feel good" thoughts, either. Very practical suggestions such as solutions to problems, names of people to contact, or books to read for guidance will pop into your head.

We discussed earlier our belief that there is no such thing as a coincidence. When you are on a mission, you become acutely aware of things around you that can be helpful in your mission. It seems that suddenly things you need appear out of the blue. Visionaries know to be vigilant, and their focus plays a role in creating the conditions that they need to succeed. If you have a clear vision for something that will benefit people on a broad scale, you owe it to yourself to trust your vision, allow inspiration to flourish, and follow it through to its implementation.

Define Your Own Time-Line

There is no defined period of time to serve before being eligible for the Visionary club. Many visionaries through history have been young when they implemented their visions. As we look around our quickly developing world, we see innovative and widely-used products appearing more frequently than at any time in history. And what separates current visionaries from those in the past is how young the visionaries are. Perhaps we have moved into an age in which the implementation of visions is more practical. Perhaps visions have always appeared to people at a young age, but in the past they may have taken a lifetime to implement. Whatever the truth, we can be grateful that we live in an era when, even in our teenage years, it is possible to implement a vision.

While it's possible that a vision can be implemented in a short time, for most visions this isn't the case. Exploring the anatomy of a successfully implemented vision reveals that the implementation does not occur all at once. It is common knowledge that failing to produce the desired outcome at the first attempt is almost to be expected. Edison tried countless variations before he perfected the conditions needed to produce the first electric light bulb.

Creating the plan to implement your vision could, in hindsight, be considered to be the moment your vision was realized. You transferred the vision from your mind to paper, giving it form. This reflects the understanding that the most likely route to implement your vision is through the gradual development of your abilities, and the continuous focus on your particular obsession.

Use Your Experience

Having developed your abilities throughout your career as identified in this book, you are in possession of considerable experience that you can channel toward the implementation of your vision. Implementing a vision will require equal doses of creativity and practical planning. Take the time to constantly contemplate in private what you want to achieve and how you will go about it. Write down what you need to do, and in what order to do it.

The result will essentially be a business plan for your vision. Be sure to include illustrations, as they will not only define your vision more clearly, they will also help you when you meet with other people who you can recruit to help you fulfill your vision.

You will quickly realize that while a vision may come specifically to you, it will take many people in different positions to see your vision implemented. You may need significant resources, both in financial and skills terms. You may need the cooperation of people in business, government, or charitable organizations. Finding these people is a key step and requires that you know a particular type of people. We call these people "Connectors".

Use Connectors

Connectors will not necessarily play an active role in implementing your vision; rather they are the people who can match you up with people who will participate actively. Connectors don't have to be high profile people in your community. You may discover that your next door neighbour, who you previously only talked to while putting out the garbage, works in an industry that has relevance to your vision. The neighbour may be able to connect you to someone who can move your cause forward.

To find these connectors, you need to put out the right signals. That might mean talking about your vision in broad terms whenever you meet with people. Equally, listening to and asking relevant questions about what other people do will yield information that could reveal that a particular person could contribute to your vision.

The wonderful thing about being a member of the human race is that most people treasure the opportunity to help someone else. This is especially true for people you already know, or for people to whom you are connected via a trusted source. Without this benefit, the evolution of our capabilities would be so slow that we would still be living in the dark ages.

When you meet people to explain your mission and gain their insight or investment, go with a positive expectation. People want to help you, and to secure that help, all you need to do is help them understand what you need and why. If people can clearly see what it is you are trying to do, they are very likely to want to work with you. If you have prepared well, and you can explain your mission in a way that they can personally relate to, you are likely to have to control their enthusiasm for your mission.

Don't Let Small-Minded People Block You

A word of warning: for a variety of reasons some people, after hearing you describe your vision, will see only obstacles. Friends are unlikely to boldly tell you that your idea is crazy. Often their objections come in more subtle ways. Perhaps they quickly formulate questions or comments that deter you, or make you second-guess your vision.

If the people you are speaking with become critical or sarcastic in their comments about your vision, politely move on to another subject. Don't disregard these comments, even the sarcastic ones, as they might be useful. But don't be put off, either.

You will discover, as you discuss your thoughts with friends— who may also become connectors—that they too have visions that they would like to implement. Encourage them and be a connector for them if you can.

Unfortunately, one of the reasons that people become critical when hearing other people's visions is that they are unable to implement their own visions. Maybe they don't feel worthy, or maybe they don't have a plan for realizing their vision. Whatever their obstacles are, you will probably recognize them when they tell you about their vision. Help them if you can. It would be a shame if, two years in the future, they were still talking about the same vision, but had made no progress.

Most people will be very happy to help you, but some people, for whatever reason, won't. Not everyone will see your vision the way you do, so don't be discouraged. Move on to the next person. After your vision is accomplished, you can be sure that those who couldn't see your vision at the beginning will happily tell others about their input to your success!

Have a Sincere Cause

Be sincere about the cause of your vision. Visions that stand the test of time and create a powerful and positive legacy for the visionary are nearly always focused toward the benefit of the broader public. If your cause is self-centred, it is unlikely to meet with success, or if it is accomplished, the legacy will be tainted. By that we mean that to have a desire to receive something, like authority, or great wealth, and then to work back to create a vision for its fulfillment is self-centred. This type of vision is unlikely to gain voluntary acceptance from those who you need to help you.

The desire to accumulate money and fame is not a cause for great achievement. It might be an effect of accomplishment, but it is not a cause. It is notable that great visionaries claim little to no interest in the money they receive from their achievements. Further, the source of their vision had nothing to do with a desire for wealth. That is not to say that any fame or fortune received for your efforts need be turned away; it is not a requirement that a visionary must live in poverty.

A sincere cause for the purpose of helping other people is likely to be well-received by those who you need to help you. Keep your vision on track with your original purpose, and don't be side-tracked by the trappings that accompany new wealth and popularity.

Don't Stop at the Starting Line

Getting started on your vision is possibly the most difficult and the most important time. It is easy to think that you are not capable, or your vision is not worthy of implementing. If that is how you think, you are right. But, imagine what the world would be like today if, at the beginning of every vision, the accompanying self-doubt took precedence. So many things that we take for granted simply wouldn't exist. Everything you use during the day began its existence in someone's mind.

It is commonly accepted that at some point in a marathon, a runner will hit a metaphoric wall. The wall is the point at which the runner feels it is impossible to continue. From that point the completion of the marathon is no longer a physical battle so much as a mental endurance test. But the marathon wall has not been experienced by everyone—why is that? Because not everyone has run a marathon.

For the many who would love to feel the accomplishment of completing a marathon, but don't participate, it is not the wall toward the end of the race that prevents them; it is the wall at the start.

Feeling the satisfaction of your vision means you must break through your wall at the start. You are likely to encounter a number of walls during your marathon, but at least you are on the course, and that's half the battle.

Have Conviction and Courage

Making the decision to start is a positive step of its own. But as soon as you put yourself on the path, the first thing you will do is look ahead, way ahead. It will be like looking up from the base of a mountain that you are about to climb and wondering how you can possibly do it. Even if you have a very well-defined map, fair weather conditions in the forecast, and an experienced team to support you, unexpected things happen. As you look up the mountain, not knowing what will happen, and when will cause most of your anxiety. If we could see in to the future and know what the outcome would be, perhaps that would eliminate any fears we might have. But, what kind of satisfaction would we derive from executing a foregone conclusion?

If we could see into the future, it wouldn't take us long to invent something that blocks our vision, just so those special few among us could feel the thrill of conquering the unknown.

But we can't see into the future, and the fear of the unknown can prevent us from moving forward. To overcome this fear takes a form of courage that separates visionaries from all those who simply have a vision. To help you develop the courage you need, keep your vision central in your mind, continually revise your plan, and remain connected to your imagination and inspiration.

Trust, that most important factor, will help you take the first step. Trust that your vision has within it the seeds of success, and that everything you need will appear just when you need it to. Visionaries have to be convinced of the value of their cause, and be courageous.

Have Patience

Although some people love change and adapt quickly, most people seem to have a natural tendency to resist any change until the new idea has been commonly accepted. This has been called the "herd mentality".

This reluctance to accept new ideas may be more than just blindly following the crowd, and it can actually serve a valuable purpose. If every idea was openly embraced and implemented, we would proba-

"Patience is no slave to time. When time is not the master, everything happens now."

bly live in a state of chaos. In the same way that a business needs to find the right balance between conformity and creativity, so too do the social systems we all live under. Most material shifts in understanding need to be tested, proven, and then gradually accepted.

Understanding and accepting the reality of slow progress is important for planning your strategy as you move forward toward your vision. It is quite possible that your enthusiasm and commitment to your cause will be strong enough to bulldoze your vision through some of the obstacles. But the bulldozer strategy is unlikely to be effective in all circumstances.

If you need to deal with any form of committee, you know from experience that there will be a process to follow, even if the outcome is known from the outset. If you need legal approval to move forward, or perhaps international agreements that require modifications to your specifications, don't ignore them and hope they will go away. Even if your cause was to bring fresh water to every human on the planet, there would still be very frustrating and often stubborn red tape to deal with, as many people continued to languish in thirst.

Patience is an important, although sometimes painfully challenging, ability that the Visionary must master.

Never Give Up

Winston Churchill after giving a speech to an assembly of school children was asked, "What is your secret to success?" He responded, "Never, never, never give up."

Navigating through process is a challenge that requires knowledge and patience. Handling objections requires information, skill, and sometimes creativity. Regardless of the size of your vision, whether it will affect the local community or the global community, there will be obstacles. Of that you can be sure. There may even be serious complications that cause you significant discomfort. The intensity of your commitment to your cause will be tested by the severity of the obstacles you face.

As we have discussed before, your commitment can create the conditions that will provide you with the answers and resources that you need, when you need them. Sometimes, the answers will not be in the form that you were expecting. For example, you might think you need a certain resource, and that becomes your focus. By looking for what you think you need, you might overlook the objective, which is to complete a task. It might be possible to complete the task in a different way. So you didn't get the resource you thought you needed, but the task got done anyway.

Be on the lookout for these occasions; once you become accustomed to resources appearing in unexpected forms, you will start to look more creatively for the possible ways, and the different resources, you need to complete your vision.

Commitment to your vision is a must. If you remain convinced of the value of your mission and aware of your surroundings, any obstacle can and will be overcome.

Release Your Shackles

To become fully committed to the successful implementation of your vision, you must release the ordinary shackles that people have. Some of your shackles will be intangible, and some will be tangible. Common shackles include: feeling unworthy, inertia, misguided loyalty to another cause, and procrastination. Maybe you will have to go without certain material comforts to support your vision, such as missing some family events or leaving your current employment. A time will come when you will clearly know what your shackles are, and you will have to decide whether to remove them and go forward, or not.

To fulfill any purpose of significant importance, you will, at some point, have to go beyond the point of no return, such that the completion of your vision is the only option. Perhaps this is why so many highly successful entrepreneurs go bankrupt before they achieve their ultimate goals. They go beyond the point that ordinary people are prepared to venture. That is not to say that you have to create a condition that forces you into despair before you can achieve your vision, but it does describe, in some measure, the commitment that separates having a vision from being a visionary.

Deciding to let go of your comfortable surroundings and trust that your vision is worthy will be a defining point on your path to becoming a visionary. That point may come early on in the process, or it may come late in your effort. When it does, you will decide the level of discomfort that you are willing to accept if called upon, and it is likely that you will only know the answer when the time comes.

Be Passionate

The emotion required to push you to let it all go, and complete your vision at all costs, is found in the basic instinct that drives the human species to survive and to multiply. Passion is a powerful motivating force. It's like high octane fuel for your engine. People throughout history have achieved great heights and sunk to immoral lows driven by the irrepressible emotion called passion. In fact, there is a fine line between sanity and insanity; that line might be where Passion resides.

When you are passionate about a cause, there is little else you can think about. The drive to realize your objective becomes all consuming. Your energy levels increase significantly. You might become intolerant of things that don't normally bother you, because anything that doesn't help your cause is an interruption. Even eating and sleeping can become annoying.

Spending time with people who are passionate about their vision can be infectious. Providing they don't knock you over in their haste to get things done, the energy they exude is inspiring, and almost tangible.

Witnessing a person obsessed with their vision can be compared to seeing a person who has lost all sense of reality. But, if your vision is not yet reality, then maybe losing your sense of reality is what is required! With a passionate commitment to do whatever it takes to realize your vision, who or what would dare to block your path?

To expand your knowledge about how to be passionate about your work, watch this free video.
http://bit.ly/1fl9sfX

Love

It is fitting that the final ability in this book is the most powerful by far, Love. Love is an unlimited, indestructible force that we all have. Love could be defined as an unconditional desire to perform at your highest levels for the good of a cause.

The ability that we too frequently block is the ability to allow love to flow freely. We have just discussed the power that can be released when you apply passion to your vision. Passion is an emotion that can drive you to extraordinary lengths, but it is unbridled, and without love it can be like releasing a wild horse into a field. It will go wherever it wants to, and you had better not get in its way!

But love is the strongest power and it provides laser-like focus. Passion blended with love creates unlimited possibilities.

For many people, mentioning "love" and their job in the same sentence would be enough to cause uncontrollable laughter. They think, "How can I possibly love my job? It's routine and mind-numbing, and only serves to pay the rent."

Think about how different this description is from that of the visionary, who feels that every day at their job is as exhilarating as going on a first date. Which one would you prefer?

Choosing to block the love for what you do will smother a significant force that can lift you up to currently unimaginable heights. If you think, "Give me a job that I can love, and I'll give it a try", you are fooling yourself. No job holds the power of love. Love is not in what you do; it is in how you do it. You have to learn to put love into how you do your job.

If that sounds impossible to you, make it your mission to put yourself in a job in which you can release your love. If this still sounds fuzzy, feel-good, and unrealistic, then please humour us for just a moment.

Suspend your reality. Find a quiet spot, sit in a chair, put your head back, smile and gaze into space. Imagine you are in a job that gives you so much excitement that it is like releasing the playful child within you, one who doesn't even know that limitations exist.

If you took that exercise seriously, you just visited the place where your visions are waiting for you.

VISIONARY STEP SUMMARY

You now influence a broad community. You are on a mission and in a relationship with your cause. At this level, people experience you as a unique source of knowledge and want to learn from you. Your vision goes far beyond your own personal goals. You are a harbinger of change and you leave a legacy.

The table below summarizes the Visionary abilities and the behaviours associated with them.

Abilities	Positive Behaviours	Negative Behaviours
Receptive to inspiration	Open to all sources of wisdom	Too logical
Defines own time line	Knows when time is right	Continually waiting for a 'sign' to start
Uses experience	Draws from all experiences	Ignores or forgets to use own experience
Uses connectors	Identifies people who can lead to the right resources	Prefers to do it alone
Doesn't get blocked by small minds	Sees beyond negative opinions	Allows criticism from others to get in the way
Has a sincere cause	Has genuine desire to help others	Visions are self-centred
Doesn't stop at the starting line	Believes in ability to achieve vision	Has fear of failure
Has conviction and courage	Has trust in value of vision	Doesn't see vision clearly enough
Has patience	Observes protocol	Impatience leads to cutting corners
Never gives up	Continues to completion	Gets blocked by obstacles
Releases shackles	Defines and accepts costs of implementation	Deterred by potential personal costs
Is passionate	Provides the energy to drive the vision through	Energy for vision becomes depleted
Loves	Provides unconditional power to achieve the vision	Holds back from fully committing to vision

CONCLUSION

The Career Acceleration Process is a real world practical process built on experience and personal involvement. Now that you have read about it, you must take action. We have identified many key abilities that, with ongoing development, will give you control of your career. If you pay attention to your current abilities, as compared to your potential, and then commit to self-development, you will experience a difference.

Be aware that the acceleration of your career and the fulfilment of your potential are entirely in your own control. In fact, if you relinquish control to others, you run a high risk of falling short of your potential. You will live with the fear of losing your job and your ability to provide for your needs. This fear will cause pressure that will prompt you to settle for a job below your capabilities, and leave you feeling unfulfilled. We have seen too many highly capable, well-meaning people struggle in their careers when all it would take is a slight shift in their perspective to allow them to soar ahead.

Every one among us is capable of achieving all that we can conceive. The Career Acceleration Process is designed to help you take an important practical step forward in your personal development. Our belief is that there are no ordinary people. If we can help you to make strides in your career, then you may see that it is very possible to make strides in all aspects of your life. In doing so, you will become happier, healthier, and more likely to provide the very best of your unique services to your community.

Throughout this book, you have been exposed to many abilities, described and explained in a sequence designed to accelerate your career. This sequence will help you gain maximum value from the knowledge presented in this book, because you can focus on the abilities that best fit with your needs, and quickly implement your new-found knowledge.

Be honest with yourself and objectively recognize which abilities you need to develop, and which provide you with a strong position for promoting your service. This part of your progression is very important. If you are vague with your needs, you may never find exactly what you are looking for, and your progression may not occur.

Ensure that you have a thorough understanding of the content in this book. This is a vital step; people who don't understand what they receive, or who are vague in what they need to learn at the outset, may dismiss content as confusing or irrelevant. If you have a thorough understanding, you are in good shape to really benefit.

The next step is contemplation. Not everything you read will fit what you need. In the contemplation stage, you should refine the content and focus on the specific knowledge that can benefit you. After you have refined the knowledge, you are in a position to experience progress. Understanding what you need and what you have now will motivate you to apply your new knowledge.

Finally, after you have applied your new knowledge, you must continually revise it. At first your knowledge may not fit exactly into the gap that you had. Analysis and revision will remould the knowledge to your gap. As time passes, your circumstances will change and your knowledge will need revision again.

Following the steps we have outlined to go from one level of responsibility to another is simply putting into practice what good leaders do. The process is practical and very achievable. You will experience a sense of exhilaration and freedom and affect the people around you in a very positive way.

"Knowledge is power", but only when it fits your needs and when you apply it. Define your need, apply the knowledge and all of your career needs and desires will materialize.

ORIGINS OF THE 7 STEPS

A MESSAGE FROM THE AUTHORS, DAVID AND SHARON

As we came to the conclusion of writing this book, we wanted to express as clearly as we could how real world the Career Acceleration Process is. We decided that the only way we could really present the truth was by giving a short account of our careers. You will then be able to recognise where the 7 Steps originated.

We have had very diverse careers and while our stories are by no means unique, each of us has experienced success that is not common. However, we are both convinced that the kind of success we have realized should and can be more common. That is why we wrote 7 Steps to Supercharge Your Career. The book was compiled from our life experiences.

We sincerely hope you enjoyed reading the book. We wish you success and happiness in your career as you fulfil your potential.

David's Story

I grew up in a working class area of South London, England. My dad was a policeman and my mom, with time off to raise my sister and then me, worked in accounting departments. We didn't have a particularly strict environment, but my parents, while not having much money, always found ways to buy us things. Values such as honesty, loyalty and hard work were very influential in my childhood. We had plenty of arguments, but there was never any doubt about the strength of our family unit.

Education wasn't particularly important and there was never any talk about college or university. Indeed, in my mid-twenties, when I decided to go back to school for a college course, my dad asked me why I would want to do that! I had, for reasons I still don't know, a desire to work in a bank from a very early age. So when I got an interview with a fairly prestigious bank when I was still only 15, things were looking good. I got the job and left school at 16. My last day at school was on Friday and my first day at work was the following Monday. My parents were very happy with me and I suspect they thought that I would retire at 65 with all their hopes for me neatly tied up with a bow on top.

Starting Out

The bank life seemed like an extension of school to me. I did what I was told and when I left at 5:00 pm, I was free to do what I actually wanted to do. Nevertheless, things were going to plan, even though I didn't have one, and I was promoted a couple of times. Then one of those moments in life occurred that, while they seem innocuous at the time, had a profound effect on my life.

One of my dad's former police colleagues stopped by the house. It was an impromptu visit, and I happened to be home. He was working in an insurance company and when he saw me, he said something like, "You have the gift of the gab. You should come and work for me and earn a fortune." With dollar signs in my eyes, and to the total despair of my parents, I resigned from the bank to go and make my fortune.

My parents despair was not unfounded. Within six months, I was out of work, with no education, and no prospects for the future. I don't recall feeling down about it. After all, I had no obligations, and my parents weren't about to put me out on the street.

Eventually, I did find another job. It was also in insurance. This time I was collecting premiums door to door and selling policies to a working class market that could barely afford a nominal premium. This time I actually did quite well, and although I wasn't earning big money, I did have at least enough to offset my parent's burdens. It was at this time that a question popped into my head. Why is it that, while all the sales people have the same product, similar territories, the same training, the same economy and very similar educational background, some are more successful than others?

I can remember to this day the thought coming to me, but I had no idea at the time that this question would drive me to educate myself and ultimately lead me to become a highly paid executive officer of an international organization.

Inspiration

I was about 20 when I started reading. Until that point, I had only read detective stories and football journals. My quest to find the answer about success would lead me to read sales books and biographies of successful people. I joined a different insurance company and began consulting on a business to business basis. I developed a business plan of sorts, based on my reading, and before too long, I was earning good money. This is when the most important event of my life occurred. I met Julie, my future wife.

For the first time in my life I really knew a truth, Julie and I were meant to be together. Julie had a very different upbringing to mine. She came from a wealthy family and had experienced luxuries that were out of my league. But she had had a very troubled childhood and was very insecure. We complimented each other well. I gave her the security she needed, and she instilled in me a confidence to be all that I could be, which until that point I hadn't really even considered.

Self-Development

I had implemented a number of ideas that had already delivered some career dividends to me, but with Julie encouraging me I knew I had to go further. This is when another key event occurred. I won a course at work and elected to study Brian Tracy's Psychology of Achievement. The course outline matched all that I had been studying on my own, and in particular, it covered speed reading. I was not a fast reader and I figured, if I could read more I would get ahead more quickly.

That course opened my mind to possibilities that I hadn't even considered. Now, I was on a mission. From then on, whenever I was in my car, which, as a sales guy, was often, I listened to self-development tapes. Brian Tracy's program came with about five hours of tapes, and I must have heard them ten times over the next few years. I bought more of his programs and the programs of other self-development masters such as Wayne Dyer, Steven Covey, Jim Rohn, and many more. These people became my virtual mentors. I implemented ideas whenever I could, testing them and adjusting them for my needs. At one point I was the top sales guy in my company and I was being invited to functions that gave me great exposure.

I always liked helping other people, but I was still out for myself when the next learning experience hit me hard. My territory was shifted and all that I had developed was swiped away from me overnight. I was shocked and disturbed at the thought of having to start all over again in a new territory. Then the lesson hit me. I had been trying to be the best, as defined by the company. Yes, I had been developing my own abilities, but for the wrong reasons. It was all about the money, and not at all about what I really wanted to do. What I realised is: I really want to help others fulfil their potential and in doing so, I would fulfil my own. I started to do presentations to other sales guys, to help them develop their skills. I joined Toastmasters to improve my speaking skills, and I started to volunteer for organisations in my community.

Career Acceleration

I left the insurance industry, and went into the corporate training industry just after immigrating to Canada. Many people have asked me why I emigrated; the best answer I can come up with is that it seemed like a good idea at the time.

Julie and I had enough money to stay in Canada for about six months. After I failed for the second time trying to sell insurance, and when our financial deadline had passed it became urgent that I find something. I took a position as a tele-sales rep even though I was over-qualified. I took my new job in full stride, implementing all the abilities I had learned over my career. Within two years I went from sales rep to President. Over the next few years I took the company from $7M to $20M in revenue and made it a very profitable business. I stayed in this company for nearly 20 years and had the immense pleasure of working with numerous wonderful and highly intelligent people.

I don't believe in coincidence; so while I took the job because it was available, it just happened to be in the training sector. My new company exposed me to a world of helping people develop their abilities, while at the same time experiencing how to run a successful business, and help develop some great people. One of the people I met, Max, developed my business skills more than any other person, and I am grateful for all that he did for me. Ironically, it was Max who would return to the business a decade after he left and in a major executive purge, he took my job!

Over the last decade of my career, I became an Executive Vice President and then Chief Operating officer. Under the guidance of another mentor, Nick, I had the privilege of working with the leaders of companies from around the world. I learned about different cultures and how to manage leaders. I got involved in corporate governance and SOX compliance, transfer pricing, and property leases.

How could this all possibly happen for a kid from South London who left school with no formal qualifications? If I had stayed at the bank, I would be planning my retirement from the bank in about 15 years. I shifted my perspective and became aware of what abilities I needed to develop. I did what I know you can do, too.

It is my mission to reach as many people as I can, to help them be all that they can be, and live a life that is available for us all, with the right guidance.

A Vision is Born

I know that there are people who have solid reasons for why they should accept their lot and do what is expected of them. And I know they are wrong. I want to reach out to everyone who needs help and give them a path. I have always enjoyed seeing people display their service at the highest levels; a sales guy or a singer, a hockey player or a doctor, a plumber or a receptionist.

It saddens me when I see people settling for less than their full potential would allow. I will help people develop their abilities, and if I have to fulfil my mission one person at a time, then I hope rein-carnation won't slow me down too much.

~David

Sharon's Story

I always wanted to be an optometrist. When I was nine years old, I got my first pair of glasses, and the world came to life. Until I put those glasses on my face, I did not know what I had been missing. So it became my dream to help people see. But I also loved singing.

From age nine, I was on a weekly radio program called The Little Players of the Air. We also did numerous stage shows each year. Before too long I was part of a singing-guitar-playing duo called The Harmony Gals and a member of the traveling Blue Sky Revue. (I wasn't yet 12 years old!)

I grew up in Montreal, as did my parents and their parents before them. But my parents never got to go to university. They had to leave school early to work in family businesses to rebuild what their families had lost in the various European debacles of the late 1800's. My generation had no choice about whether or not to go to University. It was "Yes", and no buts about it.

My parents saw that, even as a little child, I loved to play school, and I was always the teacher. So there would be no Optometry school or Broadway for me. It would have to be McGill and it would have to be a BA leading to a teaching degree. But how would

I combine my love of teaching and performing, and still help people see? This would become clear to me, eventually.

I taught school for while in Montreal and then Toronto. But after I became a mother, I could not face little ones all day and then again at home, so I went back to school and got a Masters and then a PhD in Adult Education majoring in Psychology. The degrees were great, but I was really learning about myself. Struggling in my marriage, I could not understand how I could be married to a good man and feel so miserable. I learned about people and relationships; about life's developmental stages and about how people grow in their personal and professional lives. In the process, I came to understand that my husband and I were just very different people, and I found the strength to move on alone.

While attending graduate school and raising three young daughters myself, I maintained a small counseling practice out of my home office. I specialized in working with people who had cancer. There always seemed to be a stress connection. Women with breast cancer were struggling in difficult marriages and men with stomach or esophageal cancer were struggling with feeling powerless at work. (There could be interesting metaphors there if one were to look at it more deeply!)

D.C., my last client, changed the course of my career. As a senior executive in a large firm, he had been striving to warn the leadership of impending doom, but no one would listen. By the time he came to me, his cancer, which he attributed to stress, was very advanced. Working with him moved me so much that I closed my practice and got a job counseling within an organization. I was determined to find out what it was that dampened people spirits and made them sick. I would help them see. Then I would write about it, and show how people needed to be led in order to do really well for themselves and their organization. I would help leaders see also.

I became a counsellor for the Canadian Coast Guard and Air Traffic Control and soon was promoted to Director of Counselling for a team spanning the entire country. We developed programs that were replicated internationally, and I was called on to provide advice on people management to leaders at the highest levels of the organization.

I wrote that book about stress in the workplace, and a few more (under the names Sharon Rolbin and Serena Williamson). I also wrote poetry and music and an award-winning one-woman musical comedy. By now my vision was becoming clear. No matter what I did, whether it was organizational consulting, poetry, music, or comedy, I was helping people to see, and not only with their eyes. I realized that my goal had always been to help people see who they were and what they were here for, at whatever level of responsibility they found themselves. I wanted to help them be the best they could be and make the biggest difference they could, surmounting any obstacles that they might encounter in the process. .

In addition to living in Montreal and Toronto, I spent four years in San Francisco, where a colleague, because of my PhD and publishing experience, begged me to coach him on completing his PhD dissertation. And my company, Book Coach Press was born. For the next 10 years, I guided fledgling authors from "Inspiration to Publication". I helped them clarify and develop what that they had to share. Meanwhile I continued helping more people see by leading management seminars for various international organizations and doing keynote addresses at conferences world-wide. I even became a chapter president of the Canadian Association for Professional Speakers.

My daughters are now married with families of their own, and my career had started winding down, but I was plagued with the thought that I not yet written my magnum opus, and I did not want to do it alone. I needed input from a different mind, someone with very different work and life experiences. Then it hit me that my good friend, David Booker, would make the perfect business partner in this venture. The rest, as they say, is history. Working with David Booker has been an absolute joy. I sincerely hope that you derive as much benefit from reading this book as we did writing it.

~Sharon

Appendices

On the following pages you will find the Career Capabilities Assessment and instructions on how to interpret your scores. The Assessment is also available free online at

www.CapricornCoaching.com.

When you complete the online assessment, you will immediately receive an in-depth personalized report detailing what steps you should take to Supercharge Your Career.

 Learn how to assess your career strengths by watching this video and taking the free Career Capabilities Assessment Online.
http://bit.ly/OCxxi3

-A-
Career Capabilities Assessment

In order to generate a constructive assessment, all the questions must be answered. The more objective you are with your answers, the more valuable the assessment will be. In other words, evaluate how you currently are, not how you think you should be.

Instructions: Please indicate if you agree or disagree with each statement, and to what degree by putting an **X** over the appropriate number.

#	Question	Strongly Disagree vs Strongly Agree					
Eg	Ice is cold	1	2	3	4	5	X
1	You have clearly defined career objectives.	1	2	3	4	5	6
2.	You have a clear understanding of what you can and cannot do.	1	2	3	4	5	6
3.	People consider you an uncomplicated person.	1	2	3	4	5	6
4.	Before you start something you usually have a good idea of the best way to proceed.	1	2	3	4	5	6
5.	People rarely tell you "you are a creature of habit".	1	2	3	4	5	6
6.	You make a written list of what you intend to do each day.	1	2	3	4	5	6
7.	You are someone people can depend on.	1	2	3	4	5	6

#	Question	Strongly Disagree vs Strongly Agree					
8.	You find it easy to see things from someone else's point of view.	1	2	3	4	5	6
9.	People say you are a good communicator.	1	2	3	4	5	6
10.	You are often the one who proposes a middle ground.	1	2	3	4	5	6
11.	You volunteer, often.	1	2	3	4	5	6
12.	You welcome new challenges.	1	2	3	4	5	6
13.	You feel that there is always more than one way to solve a problem.	1	2	3	4	5	6
14.	You often seek someone's help to find a solution.	1	2	3	4	5	6
15.	You have laser focus rarely, if ever, get distracted or procrastinate.	1	2	3	4	5	6
16.	In business and in personal situations you consider yourself someone who is "always" prepared.	1	2	3	4	5	6
17.	You are resourceful.	1	2	3	4	5	6
18.	You know exactly what the company objectives are at all times.	1	2	3	4	5	6

#	Question	Strongly Disagree vs Strongly Agree					
19.	You understand the company model.	1	2	3	4	5	6
20.	You are always reviewing corporate options and often say; "How can we grow the company and expand the business?"	1	2	3	4	5	6
21.	As a manager, or if you were a manager, part of your job is to respect your staff and consider their future.	1	2	3	4	5	6
22.	You make sure that things get done.	1	2	3	4	5	6
23.	People close to you never tell you that you are critical or judgemental.	1	2	3	4	5	6
24.	You are consistent in the way that you follow your objectives.	1	2	3	4	5	6
25.	You spend equal time on customer service and operations.	1	2	3	4	5	6
26.	Even though, sometimes it might not be in your personal best interest, you communicate and support the goals of the company.	1	2	3	4	5	6
27.	You often figure out what will happen in the market as things change.	1	2	3	4	5	6

#	Question	Strongly Disagree vs Strongly Agree					
28.	You have a complete understanding of the complexities of the business.	1	2	3	4	5	6
29.	You share your ideas and ask for those of your co-workers.	1	2	3	4	5	6
30.	You have a good idea of your co-workers' expertise and always find the right person to resolve the issue.	1	2	3	4	5	6
31.	Your vision is not driven by great personal rewards.	1	2	3	4	5	6
32.	You are always willing to learn something new.	1	2	3	4	5	6
33.	You are willing to sacrifice to achieve your vision.	1	2	3	4	5	6
34.	You easily build goodwill with others.	1	2	3	4	5	6
35.	You are focused on implementation.	1	2	3	4	5	6

How to Tabulate your Score

Add up your total score for each of the five questions indicated and place that number on the blank line.

Questions 1-5   Your total Score   _____/30
Functional

Questions 6-10   Your total Score   _____/30
Collaborative

Questions 11-15   Your total Score   _____/30
Progressive

Questions 16-20   Your total Score   _____/30
Constructive

Questions 21-25   Your total Score   _____/30
Leadership

Questions 26-30   Your total Score   _____/30
Executive

Questions 31-35   Your total Score   _____/30
Visionary

Your Career Capabilities Assessment Graph

Plot your score with a dot at the correct spot on the line and join your dots.

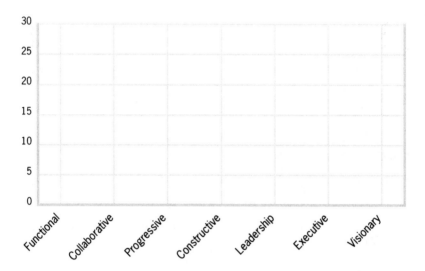

How to Interpret Your Scores

FUNCTIONAL

Higher Range: People who score in the higher range tend to be clear on who they are and what they are capable of doing. They know their work/life objectives, their strengths and weaknesses, their habits and how these habits can impact their career, and their areas that require development. They are also conscious of how to best project themselves and their services to others.

Lower Range: Those who score in the lower range may wish to ask themselves:

◊ How can I become clearer on what I am good at and what I love doing?

◊ How can I capitalize more on my strengths and develop those weak areas that may be holding me back?

◊ How am I projecting myself to others? Is lack of confidence and clarity on who I am and what I want in my career getting in my way? What can I do to address this?

COLLABORATIVE

Higher Range: People who score in the higher range tend to stick to their objectives; they work well with others and are starting to be able to influence them. They use their unique skills and abilities to provide a consistent service. They communicate well, listen, and are conscious and considerate of others. They also accept that people have different views and are flexible and tolerant. They are easy to work with and people see them in a positive light.

Lower Range: Those who score in the lower range may wish to ask themselves:

◊ How can I keep my objectives in mind and work toward them more consistently?

◊ What can I do to be sure that I am patient, listen well, and respect what the other person is saying even if I strongly disagree?

◊ Is my tone of voice and body language undermining my communication? If so, how can I make my words and actions more consistently respectful and tolerant?

PROGRESSIVE

Higher Range: People who score in the higher range have pulled ahead of the crowd. They take on additional responsibilities and start doing things that others don't. They are beginning to stand out, and people notice! People may seek them out and ask their thoughts and opinions on various business subjects. They may even find themselves being included in important cross-departmental meetings.

Lower Range: Those who score in the lower range may wish to ask themselves:

◊ How can I make the time to learn about other areas that relate to what I do?

◊ What can I do to stretch myself beyond my job description and go the extra mile?

◊ How can I be sure that when I do stretch myself, I keep in mind what the organization needs me to do, not just what I want to do.

◊ How do I deal with obstacles and criticism? Do I get defensive, feel like a victim and make the other person wrong? If so, how can I put my pride in my pocket and look for the seed of truth in what others are saying about my work, even if I do not like their tone of voice or body language?

◊ What can I do to find qualified, respected mentors whose guidance I would value and follow?

CONSTRUCTIVE

Higher Range: People who score in the higher range are still driven by their own desire to achieve, but are now also interested in the development of the business and the growth of others. They take time for reflection and are open to taking advantage of the unexpected. They move beyond their comfort zone, demonstrating their desire to find new solutions to new problems. They understand the company objectives and look for opportunities to creatively develop its products and services.

Lower Range: Those who score in the lower range may wish to ask themselves:

◊ How can I make time to contemplate how to improve myself, the business, and the people around me?

◊ What can I do to stimulate my own creativity and look for opportunities to contribute?

◊ Am I really clear on the company objectives and how the business operates? If not, how can I deepen my understanding so I can look for more opportunities to contribute on a broader scale?

LEADERSHIP

Higher Range: Those who score in the higher range are good at motivating others and managing what they do. They work for the good of the people but are also focused on productivity. They are consistent and knowledgeable. They spend time taking care of how the business runs and their business knowledge enables them to add value beyond their expected performance.

Lower Range: Those who score in the lower range may wish to ask themselves:

◊ Am I paying enough attention to both people and process?

◊ Am I able to focus on action and productivity rather than on personalities?

◊ Do I manage negativity, disagreements, and conflict efficiently?

◊ How can I ensure that I pay enough attention to both running the business and serving the customer?

EXECUTIVE

Higher Range: People who score in the higher range have earned the responsibility for the economic well-being of many people.

They work towards and communicate the company mission. They are both strategic and inspiring, and they understand both market conditions and the complexities of the business. They respect people's intelligence and although they share their thoughts and gather feedback, they often have to make the final decisions. They are able to stay true to their principles and the mission of the business, while developing the business under variable market conditions

Lower Range: Those who score in the lower range may wish to ask themselves:

◊ Am I truly committed to the mission of my organization? If not, how can I enhance that commitment, and how can I communicate it in a way that both inspires and challenges my people?

◊ How can I make my driving force more service-oriented?

◊ How can I become more informed about market conditions that affect my business?

◊ What can I do to better understand the complexities of my business?

◊ How can I maximize my respect for the people who work for me and use their intellect to the best advantage?

VISIONARY

Higher Range: People who score in the higher range influence a broad community. They are on a mission and in a relationship with their cause. They have a thirst for knowledge and are focused on implementation. People experience them as a unique source of knowledge and want to learn from them. Their vision goes far beyond their own personal goals. They are harbingers of change and may well leave a legacy.

Lower Range: Those who scored in the lower range may wish to ask themselves:

◊ What can I do to be receptive to inspiration from all sources?

◊ Am I passionately dedicated to my cause and willing to pay the price of implementation?

◊ Do I let my dreams get blocked too easily, and if so, how can I learn to push through obstacles and have the conviction, courage, and patience to see my vision through to realization.

◊ Am I so passionate, and do I love what I do, so much that working is an inspirational joy?

These results present a guide for where you are in each of the abilities measured in the assessment, and what you can focus on. For a more detailed report, please complete our free online assessment at www.CapricornCoaching.com. Contact us to find out how our experienced professional coaches can customize a program tailored to your needs.

Index

A

abilities

    areas of strength and weakness, 23

    to assess an outcome, 60

    change over time, 22

    consciously learn new, 58

    gaps in, 31

    genetic, 12

    leadership, 121, 146

    review and improve your, 58

    under-value your, 22

accomplishment, sense of, 29

achievement

    accumulation of money and fame as, 203

    of being number one, 56

    of company objectives, 144

    mistakes that propel, 59

    of objective, 105

achieving full potential, 30

acknowledging good work, 70

action, taking, 57

actions, consistency of your, 191

affirmations, 44–45

anxiety, 205

appearance, outward, 40

appetite loss, 33

area of study, expand your, 83–84

arrogance, 17, 31

ask questions, 149

attention, undivided, 67

attitude

    great, 44

managing your, 41

negative, 52, 141–43

audio books, 83

automatic pilot, 33

Auto-obedience

    about, 11, 13–16

    behaviour, disruptive, 14

    habits and, 45

    Human Middleware (HMw) and, 13, 46

B

behaviour(s)

    bullying, 16

    Constructive level, 116

    counter-productive, 17

    disagreeable, 39

    disrespectful, 47

    disruptive, 14

    entitlement, 17

    Executive level, 193–94

    influencing how others see you, 63

    leading business, 172–73

    leading people, 146–47

    negative, 17

    passive-aggressive, 17–18

    personal attributes, 36

    pre-programmed, 11 (*See also* conditioning)

    projecting yourself and your services, 51–52

    Visionary level, 211

    working with others, 73

benefit of the doubt, 125

blame, 6, 33, 45, 63, 73

blaming others, 16

body language, 68

bored, 51–52

boss, bullying, 16

boundaries, contributing beyond your, 78–79

brand, knowing your, 53–55

Brian Tracy's Psychology of Achievement, 218

Buddhist proverb, 24

business
administration, 165–66

compliance guidelines, 175

decisions, 157

development, 164

and industry, becoming an expert in your, 100–101

knowledge, 148, 170

leader, 150, 155, 169, 185

metrics, 165

mission, 179

plan for your vision, 203

positioning your, 188–89

process, refine, 170

process, reviewing, 170

purpose, 80

buy-in, implementation, 164–65

buying patterns, 169,.

C

car metaphor for business, 166

career
accelerate your, 4

blocks *vs.* development, 6–8

choices, 112

dreams and false excuses, 6

path, 4–5, 59

on purpose, 3

your, 4–6

Career Acceleration Process, 3–10,

careers of others, helping, 180

cause, having a sincere, 203–4

cause and effect, 59–60

challenge(s)
finding the, 61–62

in what you do, 62

responding to, 186–87

change course, knowing when to, 169–70

change is a fact of life, 58–59

change signals, identify, 169–70

changes, avoid making, 103–104

check-up process, 149

choice, preparing for, 112–13

Churchill, Sir Winston (British politician), 207

circumstances away from work, 97

coaching, 87, 127

coincidences, 108–9, 200, 219

collaborate with others, 69

Collaborative level, 51–73, 231–32

comfort zones, 103–5. *See also* discomfort levels

commander, being the, 176–77

commander, questions for the, 177

commit, dare to, 84–85

communication
about strategic direction of the company, 192

conflict and, 137–39

fact-to-face, 130–133

in-person, 66

listening skills, 66–68

mission success and, 188

perception of others and, 64

skills, mastering your, 65–66

of strategic objectives to employees, 176

styles of different people, 70

team spirit and, 125

technology revolution, 59

verbal and non-verbal, 67

of vision, 208

community, influence the broader, 197

community spirit, 125–26

company

objectives, working against, 169

publicly traded, 179

targets, 55

compass, setting your, 24–26

compensation, 134–135

competitive

attitude, 184

landscape, 187

complacent, 6, 189

complainer, 141–42

complete picture, seeing the, 151–53

conditioning. *See also* Human Middleware (HMw)

about, 8, 12, 71, 85, 142

pre-programmed, 8

confidence, 40, 52, 91, 101–2

conflict management, 137–39

conflicts, qualifying all side of, 137–39,

confrontational situation, 14–15

connectors, using, 202

considerate of others, being, 70–71

consistency

of decisions, 157

integrity and, 191

of notes made by hiring interviewers, 123

what you decide *vs.*, 157

of your actions, 191

of your interactions, 40

Constructive level, 97–117, 232–33

contribute beyond boundaries, 78–79

conviction and courage, 205

corporate

objectives, 188

success, climbing the ladder of, 176

courage, 205

co-workers, meeting with, 130–31

creative

being, 107

concepts, 110

use of your products, 113–114

creativity

company growth usually requires, 134–35

conformity *vs.*, 135, 206

environment that stimulates, 165

limited number of choices and, 112

objection handling requires, 207

stifled by over-built processes, 136

stimulate your, 110

creativity-conformity continuum, 136

credibility, building, 191–92

critical feedback, 139–40

criticism

accept or agree with, 138

given in private *vs.* public place, 139

negativity and, at work, 35

non-helpful, 35

people's reactions to, 32

taking it well, 39

in workplaces, 71

cultural differences

awareness of, 189–90

customer
    advocates, 113-114
    care, 165
    experience, 166
    service, 165

D
David, 56-57, 156, 186-87
David's story, 215-20
day-to-day routines, 41
deadlines, 35
decision making process, 157-59
decisions
    avoiding, 13
delegate *vs.* abdicate, 163-65
Delivery Stage, 9. *See also* Step Five—
    Leadership level; Step Six—Executive
    level
Design Stage, 9. *See also* Step Seven—
    Visionary level
desk-top, clean, 154
detail clarification, 68
Development Stage, 8. *See also* Step
    Four—Constructive level; Step
    Three—Progressive level
disagreements
    deal effectively with, 71
    internal reaction to, 71
    positively process, 71-72
discomfort levels, 207-208. *See also*
    comfort zones
Discovery Stage, 8. *See also* Step One—
    Functional level; Step Two—
    Collaborative level
distractions, 95
don't take yourself too seriously, 34-35

downside, understand the potential,
    157-59
down-swings, 169

E
educational opportunities, 83
ego-based confidence, 176-77
ego-driven approach, 56
Einstein, Albert (German-born theoretical
    physicist), 199
emergency responders, 32
employment rules, 143
encouragement, external, 28
enthusiasm, 44, 204, 207
entitlement behaviour, 17
European countries, 189
Executive level, 175-94, 233-34
executive team, 177, 182-83
experience, using your, 201-2

F
face-to-face meetings, 130-33
Far East, 189
feedback
    about objectives, 167
    asking for, 160
    critical, 139
    customer, 115
    different perspectives of, 86-87
    giving sweet and sour, 139-41
    gracefully accepting negative, 102
    HMw and, 13
    multi-dimensional, 131
    negative (sour), 139
    on oral presentations, 91-92
    of people, 30-31
    to people, 167

performance measurement and, 163

sharing thought and gaining, 192

staff, 131

work showcasing and, 92

feel good about yourself and your
    situation, 3

feeling inadequate, 71-72

fingers on the pulse, 169-70

fire fighting, 99

flexibility, 80

flippant attitudes, 34-35

focus, single-minded, 167-68

focused, staying, 167-68

focused attention, 52

full potential, short-fall in achieving, 104

Functional level, 21-49, 231

G

goal setting, 42-44

goals

    conscious of your, 112-13

    inwardly driven, 57

    to succeed, 44

gossip, 71-72, 141-42

gratefulness, 44-45, 52

gratitude, 41-42, 125

ground zero, 11-18

H

habits, 45-46

    and behaviours of successful people, 79

    knowing the impact of your, 45-47

    replacement, 47

hairstyles and dress, 39-40

happiness, 3, 44-45

Harvard MBA program, 42

health indicators, 149

help

    others, 52

    others, having the desire to, 129-30,

    someone, 203

    yourself first, 47-48

herd mentality, 206

high blood pressure, 33

high maintenance people, 127

Hillel, 69 (important Jewish religious
    leader)

hire well, 123-25

hiring interviewers, 123

hiring manager, 123-25

HMw. See Human Middleware (HMw)

home-life

    balance, 184

    balance work and, 184

how you interact with others, 65

Human Middleware (HMw). See also
        conditioning

    arrogance and, 17

    Auto-obedience and, 13

    conflicting signals from, 182-183

    definition of, 11

    habits and, 45-47

    how you interact with others and, 64

    influence experiences in, 112

    negativity and, 141

    in others, recognizing, 16-18

    productivity and, 14

    reprogramming, 15, 18, 141, 169

humour, sense of, 34-36

I

ideas, 114

    ability to present complex, 92

    arrive before their time, 110

and information, receptive to, 87

image of what you desire, create, 105–6

imagination, 199–200, 208

imperfections, recognize and work with
     your, 30–32, 39, 41

impression of how a person looks, acts,
     and performs, 67

inability to listen, 67

inaction, 57

incentive plans, 143–45

incentives, short term, 143

income, 3, 104, 144, 145. *See also* pay

incremental value, 144

independent, 42, 80, 125, 157, 180

influence(s)

   abilities and the opinions of others, 51

   abilities and your career, 58

   all humanity, 198

   broad community, 210

   cause and effect, 59

   conditioning and, 12

   control over, little, 61

   of experiences, 12

   on first class customer service, 127

   of historic visionaries, 198–99

   HMw experiences and, 112

   listening *vs.* communicating, 66–68

   lives of many people, 9

   meetings with people of, 80

   mindset and relations with people, 60

   mindset of the executive decision-
        makers, 186

   of our principles, 25

   parental, 28–29

   short-term, 132

   strategic business plans have, 178

   strategy and executives in office, 178

   of technology, 188

   of what you want to do, 100

   your behaviour and perceptions, 40

influencing how others see you, 51–63

information, impromptu, 150

information sharing down the line, 175

informed, being, 150–51

initiatives, half-finished, 163

insecure, 35, 42

insecurity, 16

inspiration, 199–200

inspire others, 54

inspiring people, 180–82, 198

intellectual growth, 100

intentions, positive, 71–72

interests, wider, 80

internally governed, 55

interruptions, 93

interview, 123–24

intimidation, 33

intuition, 199–200

IT services sector, 114–15

J

job

   perfect, 3

   productivity, 3

   satisfaction, 3

jump down their throat, 35

K

keep in the loop, 150

knowledge transfer, 85

L

label colleagues by brand, 54

leadership

abilities, 121, 146, 172

position, 121

Leadership level, 121–73, 233–34

leading

business, 148–73

from front and the rear, 156–57

people, 121–47

learning, continual, 81

learning style, preferred, 83

life's purpose, 26–27

lifestyle choices, 6, 154, 183

list of the things you are good at, 27

list writing, 153

listen, inability to, 67

listening

is key to influencing and negotiating, 71

is multi-tasking, 71

skills, 66–68

living our lives for others, 27

losing, 184. *See also* winning

love, 209–10

love what they do, 198

"low hanging fruit" problems, 170

loyalty, 177, 182

M

management team, 105, 178–79, 185

marathon, 204–5

market

competition, 184

environment, free, 184

place knowledge, 178

marketing, Internet and online, 188

marketplace, 184

material comforts, 208

McCormack, Mark H., 45

meaning, personal, 57

mediator, 137

meditation, 45

meetings

about incentive plans, 155

action items from, 159–61

agenda for, 160

with an open mind, 81

confirmation of good, 160

with co-workers, clients, suppliers, 130

to create opportunities for multi-
dimensional feedback, 131

don't call, 160

duck out of, 182

ending on time, 160

face-to-face, 130–33

feedback after, requesting, 160

follow up, 160

handouts, 159

of indeterminate length, 159

with influential people, 80

interview, 123

lacking clear and meaningful objectives,
158

material held back during, 159

message confirming key points of, 160

note taking during, 160

notes before an event or, 154

over dinner, 131

productive, 159–62

purpose of, 153, 159–60

questions, note any, 160

regional, 105

routine update, 149

sabotage, 17

social networking *vs.*, 130–31

with specific people to learn what is
happening, 149

with staff, 130

statistical analysis presentation at, 70

subject of, 159

summary of, 161

time management and, 91

tips for future, 161

well-organized, 159

well-run, 160

memories for negative reactions, 35

mental clarity, 67

mental endurance test, 205

mentor, 87

messages, non-verbal, 67

messages, unspoken, 67

micro-managing, 126, 144, 163–64

middleware (computer software), 11–12

middleware (human "software"), 12. *See also* conditioning

milestones, 151, 167–68

mindset, 61–62

creating roadblocks, 101

of organizational leaders, 40

productive, 60

miscommunication, 33

mission

focus, 53

statement, 125

your, 204

of your business, 151

mistakes, 60, 71, 125, 140

mistrust, 71

mobile device, 46, 59

modesty, 24

motivate your staff, 133–36

motivating others, 176

Murray, W. H., 86–87 (Scottish mountaineer and writer)

my way or the highway, 80

N

natural talents, know your, 28–30

negative

atmosphere, 141–43

attitude, 52, 141–43

conditions, adapt and tolerate, 103

experiences, 15

high performer, 142

person, 15, 126, 141–43

negativity, understanding the impact of, 141–43

never give up, 207

new

experiences, welcome, 81–83

ideas to fit, remodel, 114–15

solutions, problems require, 105–6

things, try, 108

nobody is perfect, 31

note taking, 111–12

notes of conversations and agreements, 111

O

obedience, unconscious, 46

object of gossip, 142

objectives

clear, 167

organizational, 38, 61, 145

personal, 82

obstacles

about, 92–94, 123, 203, 206–7

moving beyond, 92–93

for others, 71

occupational skills, 38

office chatterbox, 52

offices, international, 189–90
online studying, 84
open-minded, being, 80–81
opinions
    discounted, 15
    listen to, 40
    other people's, 30
opportunity
    for advancement, 6
    seize the, 5
optimistic, 44
oral presentation, 91–92
organization is a state of mind, 153
organizational
    fit, 53
    hierarchy, traditional, 179
    objectives, 39, 63, 147
    values, principles, and goals, 42
organized, being, 152–54, 170
outcome
    objectively analyze, 61
    responsibility for the, 61
outcomes, focusing on, 59–61
outer edge of your envelope, push the, 104
over-confidence, 154
overeating, 33
over-sensitivity, 34

P
paradigm shift, 188
paralysis by analysis, 157
parent(s)
    elderly, 184
    over-controlling, 12
    reaction to assist their child, 48
    single, 184
    taught to please our, 85

parental influence, 29
passion, 208–9
passive-aggressive behaviour, 17, 33
paths for others, improve, test and create,
    106–8
patience, having, 206–7
pay. *See also* compensation plans; income
    variable income, 143–45
people
    grow, 181
    process *vs.*, balancing the value of,
        136–37
    untrustworthy, 71
    well-meaning, 210
perception by others, 53
perceptions, 66
performance measurement, 165
persistence, 40
personal
    attributes, 22–36
    interests, 29
    mission, 69
    needs, judging someone's, 182
    problems, 45
    rights, 18
    yardstick to measure success, 43
physical tools to do the job, 162
picture of where you are headed, 78
planning
    of business functions, 185
    compensation plans, 105
    personal career goals and, 198
    of presentation, 91
    strategy for your vision, 208
    vision implementation and, 202
plans, bite-size, 60
positive

attitude, 52

intentions, 71–72

potential, achieve full, 3

praise, 139

praise from others, 101

praise in public, 139

pre-programmed

  behaviours, 11

  condition, 12

  conditioning, 8

  conscious activities, 13

presentation skills, 93–94

presentation skills, developing, 91–92

principle, pain and pleasure, 103

principles list, your, 25

process, refining, 170–71

process, reviewing and updating, 170

procrastination, 208

procrastinator, 33

product development, 188

productivity

  managing, 126–28

  targets, personal, 56

professional attitude, 72

progress *vs.* praise, valuing, 101-102

Progressive level, 77–95, 232

project managers, 162

projecting yourself and your services,
    37–49

promotion, 31

public speaking engagements, 132

purpose

  identify your, 26–28, 39

  on top of mind, 53

  at work, 101

push your envelope, 102–5

R

react defensively, 35

receptive, being, 87–89

recognition for job well done, 139

relevant, staying, 58–59

remember why, daily, 52–53

reprogramming HMw, 15, 18, 141

research your business, 100

resistance, giving clear directions to
    reduce, 128

resource allocation, 162

respect, showing, 182–83

respect for people and values, 182.

responsibility

  define level desired, 9

  desire for more, 79

  higher levels of, 79

  level below what could be achieve, 23

  level matches your potential, 3

  levels and required abilities, 7

  for the outcome, 61

  for your current career situation, 45

retail outlet, 165

rule, upside/downside, 157

S

sabotage, 15, 17

sarcastic comments, 203

sarcastic tone, 66

satisfaction, 4–5, 29, 41, 10o, 125–26, 139,
    205

seasonal change, 169

secrets, competitive, 178

seed of truth in what was said, 72

self-centred cause, 204

self-confidence, 69

self-consideration, 24

self-contemplation, 26

self-development masters, 218

self-doubt, 23, 204

self-serving element, 39

self-talk, 46

self-worth, 61

seminars, 86

senior

   management team, 179

   management updates, 150

   managers, 176, 185

serendipity, pay attention to, 108-9

service driven, 59

service-focused, 102

7 Steps origin

   David's story, 215-20

   Sharon's story, 220-22

shackles, releasing your, 207

Sharon, 68

silos of silence, 125

sleep problems, 33

small-minded people, don't let them

   block you, 202

social network, 59

social networking, 130-33

sources, cultivate reliable, 85-87

staff, motivating your, 133-36

stagnation, 59

starting line, don't stop at the, 204-5

state of chaos, 206

statistical indicators, 145

staying informed, 150

Step One—Functional level, 21-49

   about, 8, 21-22

   personal attributes, 22-36

     affirmations, 44

     behaviours, negative, 36

behaviours, positive, 36

compass, setting your, 24-26

don't take yourself too seriously,

   34-35

humour, having a sense of, 34-35

imperfections, recognize and work

   with your, 30-32

natural talents, know your, 28-29

principles list, your, 25

purpose, identify your, 26-28

stressors and reactions, know your,

   32-34

values list, personal, 25

yourself, unravelling, 23-24

powering up: projecting yourself and

   your services, 37-49

affirmations, 44-45

attitude, managing your, 39-41

behaviours, negative, 49

behaviours, positive, 49

goal setting, 42-44

gratefulness, 41-42

habits, knowing the impact of your,

   45-47

help yourself first, 47-48

transitional ability, 38-39

Step Two—Collaborative level, 51-73

   about, 8, 51

   influencing how others see you, 51-63

     abilities, review and improve your, 58

     action, taking, 57

     behaviours, negative, 63

     behaviours, positive, 63

     brand, knowing your, 53-55

     challenge, finding the, 61-62

     outcomes, focusing on, 59-61

     relevant, staying, 58-59

remember why, daily, 52–53

targets, setting personal, 55-57

working with others, 64–73

about, 64–65

behaviours, negative, 73

behaviours, positive, 73

communication skills, mastering your, 65–66

considerate of others, 70–71

disagreements, positively process, 71–72

listening skills, 66–68

trusting yourself and others, 68–69

Step Three—Progressive level, 77–95

about, 8, 77–78

working in a team environment, 77–95

area of study, expand your, 83–84

behaviours, negative, 95

behaviours, positive, 95

boundaries, contributing beyond your, 78–79

commit, dare to, 84–85

new experiences, welcome, 81–83

obstacles, moving beyond, 92–93

open-minded, being, 80–81

presentation skills, developing, 91–92

receptive, being, 87–89

sources, cultivate reliable, 85–87

tasks, managing, 89–91

Step Four—Constructive level, 97–117

about, 8, 97–98

behaviours, negative, 117

behaviours, positive, 117

business and industry, becoming an expert in your, 100–101

choice, preparing for, 112–13

creative use of your products, 113–14

new ideas to fit, remodel, 114–15

new problems require new solutions, 105–6

note taking, 111–12

paths for others, improve, test and create, 106–8

progress *vs.* praise, valuing, 101–2

push your envelope, 102–5

serendipity, pay attention to, 108–9

thinking, taking time for, 98–100

thoughts, capture your, 109–10

Step Five—Leadership level, 121–73

leading business, 148–73

about, 148

behaviour, negative, 173

behaviour, positive, 173

business in data terms, knowing the, 149–50

change course, knowing when to, 169–70

complete picture, seeing the, 151–53

decision making process, apply a, 157–59

delegate *vs.* abdicate, 163–65

focused, staying, 167–68

informed, being, 150–51

leading from the front and the rear, 156–57

meetings, having productive, 159–62

organized, being, 153–56

process, refining, 170–71

success, being a resource for, 162–63

two sides of the business, working on, 165–67

leading people, 121–47

behaviours, negative, 147

behaviours, positive, 147

conflicts, qualifying all side of, 137–39

face-to-face meetings, 130–33

feedback, giving sweet and sour, 139–41

help others, having the desire to, 129–30

hire well, 123–25

negativity, understanding the impact of, 141–44

people *vs.* process, balancing the value of, 136–37

productivity, managing, 126–28

resistance, giving clear directions to reduce, 128–29

staff, motivating your, 133–36

targets, setting beneficial, 143–45

team spirit, creating, 125–26

Step Six—Executive level, 175–94

about, 9, 175–76

behaviours, negative, 194

behaviours, positive, 194

business, positioning your, 188–89

challenges, responding to, 186–88

commander, being the, 176–77

competitive, staying, 184–86

credibility, building, 192–93

cultural differences, demonstrate awareness of, 189–92

inspiring people, 180–82

respect, showing, 182–84

strategic, being, 178–80

Step Seven—Visionary level, 197–211

about, 9, 197–98

behaviours, negative, 211

behaviours, positive, 211

cause, having a sincere, 203–4

connectors, using, 202

conviction and courage, 205–6

experience, using your, 201

inspiration, being receptive to, 199–200

love, 209–10

never give up, 207

passion, 208–9

patience, having, 206

shackles, releasing your, 207–208

small-minded people, don't let them block you, 202–203

starting line, don't stop at, 204–5

time line, defining your own, 200–201

visionary, defining, 198–99

step forward, 78

strategic

being, 178–80

direction of company, 151

objectives, 124, 150

plans, 178–79

stress from disorganization, 153

stress reduction, 154

stressful situations, 34

stressors and reactions, know your, 34–36

subconscious mind, 46

subject-matter expert, 92

success(ful)

abilities and how your fit in an organization and, 53

achievement of an objective, 107

applicant, 123

arrogance and intimidation affect, 33

being a resource for, 162–63

benchmarks to measure, 93

business and skill sets, 163

care spent on running your business and, 170

career, 4–5, 43, 53

career path and, 5

cause is congruent with the mission, 178

communication and, 188

communication skill and, 65

in corporate life, 37

cultural diversity and, 183

in dealing with your boss, 16

dependent on the will and actions of
　　　others, 43

in different aspects of life, 26–27

doesn't happen by accident, 5

doing your best to make a difference, 79

goals and plans to achieve, 43

goals ensure, 43

from having the right people with the
　　　right skills, 136

with high level of responsibility, 121

influencing how others see you and, 64

innovative process to achieve, 107

inspiration and, 217

inspiring people and, 170

ladder of corporate, 176

leader, 121

long term, 167

measurable processes and, 136

models in other countries, 189

negative attitude and, 141

outcome and clear task parameters, 164

people, habits and behaviours of, 80

personal yardstick to measure, 43

plan to achieve your goals and, 43

position of your business, 188

project resources and, 162

purpose to achieve and, 128

reprogramming HMw for, 142

resources for, 163

sales person, 56

seek and accept input from others for,
　　　87

self-centred cause *vs.*, 204

strategic objectives communication
　　　and, 178

target setting and, 55

task analysis and, 89

team goals and, 143

testing new methods and, 108

verifying new approaches for, 107

vision implementation, 198, 201, 203,
　　　208

what makes you tick and, 22

what people think and say as barometer
　　　of, 177

what you can do and how you are
　　　perceived by others and, 22

from what you give *vs.* receive, 101

winning and, 184

Winston Churchill (British politician
　　　and Prime Minister) and, 207

suggestion, stimulating, 87

T

talent, natural, 30

talent development, 129

targets

　company, 55

　compensation-based, 143

　personal, 55

　setting beneficial, 143–45

　setting personal, 55–57

　variable income-based, 144

task management, 89

tasks

　autonomy to complete, 163

delegating some of your, 163

irrelevant, 136

managing, 89–91

right people for the, 163

team spirit, creating, 125–26

think outside the box, 29

thinking

about yourself, 23–24

purposeful, 100

taking time for, 98–100

thoughts

capture your, 109–110

productive, 57

question your, 110

time between tasks, 52

time line, defining your own, 200–201

time management, 89

tolerance of others, 39

tone of voice, 67, 71

top performers, 144

top shape mentally and physically, 48

training, 6, 31, 91, 100, 126, 163, 184, 217–18

transitional ability, 38–39

trust yourself, 68

trusting yourself and others, 68–69

trustworthy, 39, 69

two sides of the business, working on, 165–67

U

UK business, 105–6

uncomfortable, do the, 104

unconscious obedience, 46

under-achievement, 100

United Kingdom, 189

unworthy feeling, 208

upside/downside rule, 157

V

value, incremental, 144

values, identify your, 25

values list, personal, 25

variable component of pay, 144

variable income pay, 143–45

victimization of the staff, 17

views of others, differing, 182

visionaries, 197–99

visionary, defining, 198–99

Visionary level, 197–211, 234–35

volunteer

for additional duties, 82

W

walk the office or workplace, 150

walk-about, 150

wealth, desire for, 204

What am I good at?, 27

What do I love?, 27

What do my skills offer to others?, 27

What does the world need?, 27

What gives me satisfaction when working with other people?, 29

What They Don't Teach You at Harvard Business School (McCormack), 42

what you think about what you do, 65

wheel, reinvent the, 105

Why do we do things this way?, 97

winning, 184. *See also* losing

winning at all costs, 184

win-win scenario, 71

win-win situation, 143

work commitment, 184

work habits, 54

working

   environment, 80, 102, 177, 183, 185, 189

   environment, unpleasant, 103

   with others, 64–73

   relationship, constructive and

      beneficial, 15

   in a team environment, 77–95

workplace

   challenges, 35

   conversations, 48

   fear, 17

   values and principles, 25

writing thoughts on paper, 109–110

Y

yourself, unravelling, 23–24

To help you fully integrate the Career Acceleration Process into your work routine, we have created a mobile seminar series for you.

To find out more about the Career Acceleration Process mobile seminar series or to find out about career development coaching, please go to

CapricornCoaching.com

Added Value

 To learn about our Book Buyer Bonus and get free access to a career acceleration portal that is loaded with free success tools, go to
http://bit.ly/1dtdPLW

**http://capricorncoaching.com/
insight/book-buyer-bonus**

CPSIA information can be obtained at www.ICGtesting.com
Printed in the USA
LVOW09s0037260814

400824LV00028B/1033/P